I, The Lord God
Say Unto Them

The Great Awakening Volume IX

Sister Thedra

ISBN: 978-1-7363418-5-8

Dedicated to those who seek The Light which never fails

Contents

Mission Statement

Give the truth to the world. Let it be received where it will. Many will read the messages. Some will accept the truth, others will read through curiosity, a few will ridicule. Yet to all is the truth given, and to all remains the power of choice.

The hope of the world in these times is in spiritualizing all forms of activity---promoting understanding through love and service. These must be the watchwords if the world is to come into lasting peace. We are trying to influence a world that is going astray and could cause undreamed of suffering. We are trying to overcome the thought of materialists and to bring a spiritual outlook into the earthly life. We need the help of all on earth who can think in spiritual terms. The great battle to be fought now is between the spiritual and the material, between idealism and carnalism. You can help by spreading the word---we are asking that you help because the battle may be long and the victory far away.

Halls of Light is not allied with any sect, denomination, political entity, organization, neither endorses nor opposes any cause. There are no dues for membership. Halls of Light is self-supporting through its own voluntary contributions. Halls of Light has but one purpose: to help through encouragement and understanding...

To contact the publishers or to obtain copies of our other books, please contact us at email: goldtown11@gmail.com

About the Late Sister Thedra

Since the later part of the last Century the Kumara wisdom preserved by Aramu Muru has begun to reemerge into the world. This process began with the late Sister Thedra, whom Jesus Christ appeared physically to while on her deathbed and spontaneously healed her of cancer while she was in the Yucatan, where she had gone to accept her fate, and the will of our Lord Jesus Christ. That is when something miraculous occurred.

Jesus spoke to her saying, "My name is Esu Sananda Kumara" and then sent Thedra down to the Monastery of the Seven Rays to learn the Kumara wisdom.

After five years, Thedra was told to return to the United States where she founded the Association of Sananda and Sanat Kumara at Mt. Shasta in California. While heading this organization, Thedra channeled many messages from Sananda and taught the Kumara wisdom until her passing in 1992.

While in the Yucatan it is said that while Sister during the 1960s Thedra was in the Yucatan, she was told a secret by her friend George Hunt Williamson, also known as Brother Philip, who authored Secrets of the Andes, and the SECRET PLACES OF THE LION. Williamson, confided in his long-time friend Sister Thedra that he intentionally scrambled the reincarnational lineages in order to protect this next generation when they the Mayan Solar Priests, who were the direct line descendants of the Kumara according to prophesy were scheduled to reincarnate or return to fulfill their missions upon Earth, one of which was to relocate these ancient sites where the original records of the Amaru were placed for safe keeping.

Sister Thedra, 1900-1992, spent five years at the abbey undergoing intensive spiritual training and initiations. While in South America in the Yucatan, she had an experience which changed her in an instant when as it is told by her that Jesus Christ physically appeared to her and spontaneously cured her of cancer.

He introduced himself to her by his true, name, "Sananda Kumara," thereby revealing his affiliation with the Venusian founders of the Great Solar Brotherhoods. It was by his command that Sister Thedra went to Peru where in here travels she met Williamson. Sister Thedra eventually left Peru upon telling her experience there was complete.

Even before she returned to the States she met with harsh criticism from the church, which she elected to leave. (JW That was the church that is in Salt Lake City, Utah.)

She then traveled to Mt. Shasta in California and founded the Association of Sananda and Sanat Kumara. A.S.S.K.

You ask, Is There A Difference Between Jesus and Sananda?

Our Lords name given at birth by his father Joseph, and his beloved mother Mary was Yeshua, thus being of the house of David and the order of Yoseph, he would be called Yeshua ben Yoseph.

The Roman Emperors placed the name of Jesus upon the sir name of Yeshua, after the Emperor Justinian adopted Christianity as the official faith of Rome, and ordered that the sacred books be compiled, upon approval of a specially appointed council, appointed by the Emperor, into a recognizable and uniform work titled The Bible. Prior to this there never was a Bible per se.

There existed until the time of the Emperor's edict, a selection of many Sacred texts, that were employed in the Sacred Teachings. Many of which were copies of what the Greeks had transposed from the original texts in the Libraries of Alexandria, which were originally compiled by Alexander the Great, and were destroyed by Julius Caesar, fearing that they might prove dangerous to the rule of a Caesar, an Earthly God.
In addition, it kept. (he thought) the knowledge of Alexander's Libraries, out of the hands of the Ptolemy's, who were said to be descended from his bloodline.
At the time Caesar had no way of knowing the vast portions of the Library that were already in the Americas, in the Great Universities of the Inca, and the Maya.
Yeshua spent many years in the East after his ascension.
The good Sheppard, upon his appearances to the

Apostles after his ascension told his Apostles that he was in fact going to tend to his Father's other sheep; which means, plainly that he was continuing upon his sacred journey.

As the ascended one, Yeshua took to himself the name of Sananda, meaning the Christed one, and Sananda was thus embraced forever more by the Great Solar Brotherhood.

To many of you this is all new, to others it will be received as a welcome easing of the wall that has so long separated two sides of the same coin, this is being placed into the ethers and the matrix of thought at this time as it is the time of the Awakening, and the Christos is already emerging into the new consciousness, and mother Earth herself.

Sister Thedra and the phenomenon of channeling. Authority to use the name of Sananda was given to Sister Thedra when Jesus~ Sananda appeared to her in the Yucatan, and cured her instantly of the cancer that had taken her body over. Further, he allowed a picture of his countenance to be taken at that time that she might realize the occurrence was more than a dream. (JW I was told by my teacher and Guru Merelle Fagot that Thedra had a large format camera called a 620, if I remember right, and it had bellows on it and founded out. She used this to take the picture of Sananda. Merele said that she got some real good pictures with that camera. I have seen this picture that Thedra took and Sananda didn't look very handsome, he just looked like a normal person with not too long of hair and he had very dark skin.) Sanada's Message to her by Sister Thedra.

"Sori Sori: Mine hand I have placed upon thine head, and I have given unto thee the authority to use Mine name. Give unto them the name Sananda, by which they shall know Me as the Lord thy God - the Son of God, sent that ye be made to know me, the One sent from out the inner temple that there be Light in the world of men."
(The meaning of "Lord God: "The Lord God, for he is "Lord" of, and responsible for, that which he has brought forth.)

"Now it is come when ones which have the will to follow Me shall come to know Me by that name which I commanded thee to give unto the world as Mine "New name."
There are many that shall call upon the name of Jesus, yet, they will deny the new name as they are want to do. While unto thee I give assurance that I am the One sent that there be Light in the world of men. Now let this be understood, that they that deny Mine New Name deny Me by any name. So be it I have appointed thee Mine spokesman; I've given unto thee the power and authority to speak for being that which I AM. And I say unto thee Mine child whom I have called forth and anointed thee with the Holy Spirit, thy name shall be as it is now called, Thedra - that name I spoke unto thee from out the ethers, and thou heard Me and accepted that which I gave unto thee; and wherein have I deceived thee? Wherein have I forgotten thee, or left thee alone?"
"I say unto thee, Mine hand is upon thee and I shall

sustain thee and you shall come to know that which I have kept for thee. So be it that I have kept thy reward, and at no time shall it be dissipated of scattered, for it is intact. So let this Mine Word suffice them which question thee - let them question, and I shall bear witness for thee. For do I not know
  Mine servants from the traitor?
Do I not reward Mine servants according unto their works or merits? I speak that they might know that I am mindful of Mine servants, that I am not a poor puny priest who has forgotten his servants."

"I say unto them, Mine servants shall be glorified above the crowned heads of the nations which have set themselves apart, and denied Me Mine part of Mine word for they have turned from Me in their conceit and forgetfulness."
"Now let this go on record as Mine Word, and I shall give unto them proof, which are of a mind to follow Me. So be it as I have spoken and I am not finished; I shall speak again and again, and I shall rise Mine Voice against them which set foot against Mine servants, and they shall be as ones cast out. So let them ask of Me and I shall enlighten them. So be it I know where of I speak. Be ye as ones blest to accept Me and know Me for that which I AM.
The Final Messages
On Saturday, June 13, 1992, at exactly 10.00 PM, at the age of 92, Sister Thedra made her final transition from the comfort of her own bed. When the time

arrived, she simply took one small breath and slipped quietly away, without pomp or fanfare.

She left as she had lived...as a humble servant for the greater good.

The messages that follow were given to Sister Thedra shortly before her transition.

They are compiled here to give you some idea of the significance of her passing and of the expansion of the work, as she is now free to work unencumbered by the physical limitations and by the pain which has so encumbered her in the past.

She has carried on the work here on the Earth plane for the last 50 years because that's where the work was needed...rest assured that her work now in the higher realms will simply be an extension of that work.

Introduction

Hope in a time of dim hopes, comfort in a time of great stress, clarity in a time of confusion, and a restatement of the primacy of the Creator over His creation--these are some of the qualities to be found and treasured in this volume of messages written down by Sister Thedra.

The messages found in the language of the early English Bible an appropriate medium which carries both their extreme simplicity and their great weight; indeed, this is not light reading. We are invited to join Sister Thedra in her communion with those representatives of Deity which are her close and dear companions. In order to sense the validity of these offerings, we must move toward the consciousness from which they emanate, and the consciousness which received them. This is a strenuous spiritual exercise, which not all will welcome. Those who do will be richly rewarded.

In the spiritual life, the qualities or unique energies of consciousness are the message, ultimately. What is qualitatively inspiring, uplifting, blissful, strengthening, loving, transforming and humbling is real and true. This is not a matter of information per se. It is a matter of the interception and translation of levels of awareness and consciousness not contacted in mundane human life. This is the substance of all true prophecy and revelation.

In these days of renewed interest in psychics, mediums, telepaths, and "channels" of all kinds, it is important to qualitatively distinguish origins and therefore the relative value and merit of what is received. Only the utmost discipline of daily life and personal consciousness, coupled with great and prolonged striving and deep humility, can put one en rapport with the high consciousness of the aspects of Deity and its Emissaries. It is, indeed, a process of communion and of identity, first with one's own inner divinity, and through its mediation, with still more profound levels of being.

In her own life and to those about her, Sister Thedra demonstrates these qualities unreservedly and without qualification. For this reason, she has earned the right and the responsibility to perform her tasks as prophetess and scribe. Many there are who will scorn, doubt and question--and have done so. Great will be their loss. For seldom, and not without lengthy preparation, do the great Beings recorded here communicate directly with humanity. It is the measure of their appropriateness to the times that these transmissions, which have served as study papers within the Mission of Sister Thedra, are now to be available in published form. May we give full attention to the admonitions, accept unreservedly the blessings bestowed as our own, and help fulfill the stated requirements for a better time.

Most of all, may we approach our responsibilities as they are shown to us with the same wholeness of being and joyful acceptance as has the recipient and compiler of these messages.

Donald Keys

Authority to Use The Name Sananda

Sori Sori: Mine hand I have placed upon thine head, and I have given unto thee the authority to use Mine Name. For 1 first showed Mineself unto thee with the Word: "Go feed Mine sheep. Give unto them the name Sananda, by which they shall know Me as the Lord God - the Son of God sent that ye be made to know Me - the One sent from out the inner Temple that there be Light in the world of men."

Now it is come when the ones which have the will to follow Me shall come to know Me by that Name which I commanded thee to give unto the world as Mine "New Name". There are many which shall call upon the name of Jesus, yet they will deny the New Name as they are want to do. While unto thee I give the assurance that I am the One sent that there be Light in the world of men. Now, let this be understood, that they which deny Mine New Name deny Me by any name. So be it that I have appointed thee Mine spokesman; I've given unto thee the power and authority to speak for being that which I am, and I say unto thee Mine child whom I have called forth and anointed thee with the Holy Spirit, thy name shall be as it is now called Thedra - that name I spoke unto thee from out the eth, and thou heard Me and accepted that which I gave unto thee; and wherein have deceived thee? Wherein have I forgotten thee, or left thee alone?

I say unto thee, Mine hand is upon thee and I shall sustain thee and ye shall come to know that which I have kept for thee. So be it that I have kept thy reward, and at no time shall it be dissipated or scattered, for it is intact. So let this Mine Word suffice them which question thee - let them question, and I shall bear witness for thee. For do 1 not know Mine servants from the traitor? Do I not reward Mine servants according unto their works or merits? speak that they might know that I am mindful of Mine servants, that I am not a poor puny priest who hast forgotten his servants.

I say unto them, Mine servants shall be glorified above the crowned heads of the nations which have set themself apart, and denied Me Mine part of Mine Word - for they have turned from Me in their conceit and forgetfulness.

Now let this go on record as Mine Word, and I shall give unto them proof, which are of a mind to follow Me. So be it I have spoken and I am not finished; I shall speak again and again, and I shall raise Mine Voice against them which set foot against Mine servants, and they shall be as ones cast out. So let them ask of Me and I shall enlighten them. So be it I know whereof I speak. Be ye as ones blest to accept Me and know Me for that which I am.

Sananda

Given to Sister Thedra

Saturday, 10:30 p.m.

September 26, 1975

Sananda

"Mine Son"

-Solen Aum Solen

O - Holy art Thou Mine Son - Mine Son which I have named Sananda - by Divine Right. He Mine Son cometh unto Me as Mine First Born. I give unto Him the Name from the beginning of His sojourn upon the planet Earth - 1 give it Him in remembrance.

I speak of Mine Son as the "First Born" - for is He not?

I say unto thee: He, Mine Son, the One I have given the Name Sananda, hast now come unto Me on thine behalf, that He might have greater - yet greater concourse with thee; that ye might be as ones prepared to enter into HIS place of abode. I ask of thee nothing save obedience unto the law; and walk ye after Him, Him which I have sent unto thee - that ye might return unto Me with Him, Mine Son Sananda.

I speak unto thee in His Presence, that ye might bear witness of Mine Word. I tell thee as He would, that thou art the ones called out from amongst them; that the Order of Melchezedek be fortuned thine service, which is as none other at this time. For this have I called thee, and thou hast answered: "Here am I." I have not denied thee; I have not cut thee off from Mineself.

I bid thee enter into the Holy of Holies, and partake of Mine Substance, O Holy Ones of Israel. Walk ye after Him, Mine Son

Sananda, and pass into the Inner Temple as ones purified and justified.

I AM Solen Aum Solen

Esu Jesus Sananda

This reproduction is from an actual photograph taken on June 1st, 1961, in Chichen Itza, Yucatan, by one of thirty archaeologists working in the area at the time. Sananda appeared in visible, tangible body and permitted His photograph to be taken.

Sananda's Appearance

Be ye as one which hast heard Mine Voice and responded unto it - for I speak that ye hear, and I say that which is wise and prudent.

Let it be known that 1, the Lord thy God hast spoken and bear ye witness of Me, for I have made manifest Mineself that ye might know Me - and for this wast these manifestations made.

I say that I have made Mineself manifest that ye might see Me with thine mortal eyes; that ye might bear witness of Me. Yet thine companions saw and believed not; neither did they hear, for they were selfish and unprepared - yet, did I deny them?

I say; I came that they which would might see and hear. I went and came again unto Mine own. So be it that I have found; I have given unto the found that they which know not might know; that they might come to know as thou knowest.

Yet, how many hast turned from Me and persecuted thee for Mine Word. It is said, "Woe unto them which persecute Mine servants." is it not the law which they set into motion?

Yea Mine beloved, I say they bring about their own downfall. So be it that I am a compassionate one, and I would that they know what they do. So be it they shall learn well their lessons. So let it be, for this is the mercy of God, the One which hast sent Me.

So be it. I AM the Wayshower, the Lord thy God

I AM Sananda

BE SURE OF THE GROUND

Sanat Kumara Speaking:

I am the authority for that which I give unto thee, and I am responsible unto none other - for I am qualified by Divine Right to speak unto thee on this subject, which is "Preparedness".

For this hast the Earth given unto thee habitation; a place wherein ye might prepare thineself for thine return unto thine dwelling place.

I say unto thee, thou art wanderers within the Earth, clothed in dense matter, crude in form and size - crude matter.

While it hast been said that it weighs heavy upon thee, it is so - and so shall it be. Yet thou art not bound by the flesh; thou art not confined to flesh, for thou art Spirit.

Spirit is not limited to form, place, or time. These are trappings of thine own limitations.

I say, these are of "Time", and time shall pass as the shadows with the noon-day sun, for it is but the illusion of the ones "bound" in flesh.

"Time" belongs to the world of physical matter, dense matter, and it shall be as naught in the real wherein ye shall know as I know.

I say unto thee, be ye as ones which can be as the eagle; soar with Me; come and be as ones which can comprehend things of Spirit.

1

Let not thine dogmas, creeds, opinions, customs, and "righteous beliefs" deter thee from the strait and narrow way which is the way of TRUTH.

Let not the creeds of man turn thine head. Harden not thine heart; forge not thine legirons; I tell thee of a surety; they shall be unto thee thine own undoing.

I say unto thee, "Listen unto that which Spirit sayeth," and be ye as ones led aright. Cast aside all thine old preconceived ideas, and take thine fingers out of thine ears, and turn from all thine sorrows and woe, and they shall be as nothing, for they are but the stepping stones.

I say, pick up thine feet and place them on higher ground; yet, ye shall be sure of thine footing, for there are ones which would lead thee into dangerous paths wherein ye could be trapt.

I say, "Be ye sure of the ground," and be ye alert. For this is it said: Be ye as one responsible for thine ownself; ye shall choose which way ye shall go. Yet it is said, "Choose ye wisely". For this do I now speak out that ye might be prepared to know the true from the false.

Seek ye the Light, and it shall be given unto thee, and no man shall lead thee into the trap.

Heed ye Mine words and be ye as ones wise, for come from the real ye know not. I am sent as One of the Mighty Council that I might add Mine Light unto that of Mine beloved Brother Sananda - yea, and Mine beloved Sister which is Mine hand made manifest in this Mine word unto thee - for by her grace is it made possible that I speak unto thee thusly.

So be it. She too is blest even as I am blest.

I AM Sanat Kumara

OBEDIENCE

Sori, Sori,

In this wise shall i speak unto thee; in this wise shall | speak unto them which are of a mind to learn of Me. And they which are of a mind to hear that which I say unto them shall profit thereby.

At no time shall I mislead them which follow Me, for I shall lead them aright. And at no time shall I suffer them to be led astray - yet they shall be of a willing mind, and they shall come of their own will.

I say unto them, "COME," and they which come shall receive of Me, and they shall be blest.

Hear Me, and give unto them as I give unto thee for them. Yet ye shall add nothing to, neither take away one jot or tittle.

Ye shall be as Mine hand made manifest - as Mine Voice - and I shall put words into thine mouth, and I shall give unto thee comprehension of that which thou sayest - for I am the author and the finisher of Mine work. And at no time shall I deny thee, for I say, I have appointed thee Mine handmaiden, and thou hast served Me well. Yet, I now have a part for thee which shall be brot about by and thru thine obedience unto Mine Voice, and ye shall be as one rewarded. So be it. I shall speak unto thee again in greater measure.

I am now prepared to give unto thee in greater capacity.

I AM Sananda

THE COMMAND

Be ye as the Voice of Me and speak the words which I put into thine mouth - and for this shall ye find favor with Me, for I shall give unto thee in great measure, and I shall not deny thee.

I shall fill thine cup to overflowing, and I shall not deny thee.

I say, ye shall be as Mine Voice and Mine hand made manifest unto them which seekest the Light which I am. For this have I prepared thee.

Now ye shall do a mighty work, and ye shall fortune unto thineself great joy. Peace, Peace, Peace - Mine Peace I shall give unto thee. Let it be Mine Peace, for this is thine reward.

I AM Sananda

ON REBELLION

Holy - Holy is the Word of God. Holy - Holy is the Name of Solen Aum Solen.

Holy is the WORD, and I shall speak the Word and ye shall record it as I speak it, for thou shall hear it, and it shall be written as thou hearest it. And not one word shall be out of place or out of order, for I shall so order it that it shall be liken unto the order in which I have spoken it. And no man shall undo Mine work, neither shall he improve upon it.

Now I say unto thee Mine beloved: Thou shall begin a new work and a new part - and for this hast thou waited. Let it be said, that in Mine own time I shall bring forth one to do Mine work; and it is now time that Mine work be done in such manner as I decree. So be it that I have decreed this be done at this time, and thou art Mine chosen vessel for this Mine part which I shall now give unto thee. It shall be given in parts, and then they shall be assembled together, that they make up one parcel of the whole.

I say the parts of portions shall be put together as one parcel or part of the whole.

Now ye shall assemble thineself together as before, and as one of body, mind and spirit; and ye shall be as one in spirit, and I shall give unto thee a portion - each one at a time, and one at a time. And for this have I said: "Be ye as ONE" for it is now come when there is one prepared. It is profitable unto Me, and any discord I shall remove, for I am not favorable unto discord.

I am within Mine right to ask obedience unto the law; and at no time shall I be obliged to tolerate rebellion in Mine house. I say rebellion is no part of Mine servants, for they are not of a mind to rebel. I say that I am not a task master; yet I say, too, that I demand obedience unto the Law. Be ye as ones blest, and I shall place Mine hand upon thine head, and I shall anoint thine head with oil, and ye shall find peace.

So be it I shall speak later.

Sananda

THE SEVENTH VIAL IS OPEN

Be ye this day prepared to proceed with Mine Work, for I am the Lord thy God which speaketh unto thee for the good of ALL - So be it as The Father wills it.

I have prepared thee as a fit vessel to receive this Mine Word, and I have poured out upon thee Mine Spirit, and I have ordained thee Mine Holy Minister. I have set thee apart from them for thine obedience unto Me, for I find in thee no rebellion and no guile. I find thee a willing servant and a dutiful one.

Now ye shall do that which I shall give unto thee to do, and ye shall be as one prepared. For this hast it been said, "As thou art prepared, so shall ye receive," it is so, according to the Law.

Ye shall place within Mine hand thine, and I shall lead thee every step of the way - so be it I shall lead thee aright. Write that which I say unto thee that they might also be prepared to receive of Me, and that they might open up their hearts unto Me, that I might dwell therein.

Let no man turn thee aside, neither seek ye favor of man, for man hast not yet reckoned with the Host. They know not the power of the Word; neither hast man seen the GREAT POWER OF THE HOST. I say unto thee: Power is Theirs and They misuse it not.

Blest are they which doth receive of the Mighty Host, and the Host now stands ready to pour out the Seventh Vial. I say, the Seventh Vial is open, and it shall be poured out upon a people, and that people shall stand as witness of the power of The Host, for they shall receive of the Vial which I hold within Mine hand.

The time is now at hand when all which are obedient unto the law - which are as willing servants - shall be anointed with the Holy Spirit, and these shall I give Mine Peace, and I shall bring them out of bondage. For these shall I give a portion, and they shall be as the ones which have earned their passport into the place of Mine abode.

Ye shall be as one which hast earned thine, for none enter empty-handed. Thou comest into Mine place of abode with all that thou art; all that thou hast thou bringeth with thee. Yet I say, none come bringing with them the gangrenish elements of Earth; these which are the stench in Mine nostrils - the desires of flesh and the want of flesh. I say unto thee: Man's offal shall be as naught in Mine place of abode. I say: First, he shall cleanse himself; he shall empty out all that is not of Me; all that is impure; and he shall enter clean and purified. Then he shall be justified by Me, for I know that which he is · that which he hast become.

Ye shall be as one purified, then I shall say unto thee: "Pass ye in and abide with Me forevermore" - rejoice ye that thou hast received thine passport.

Let them which have ears to hear, hear that which I say unto them, and I shall speak unto them in language simple and as one knowing their needs.

I say, they shall empty out the old wine - for have they not drunken of its dregs and become as ones drunken; as ones inebriated? They are indeed drunken! Drunken, I| say! They are as

9

ones filthy! For they have partaken of all sorts of abominations; they have wallowed in the pig sties; they have forfeited a prince's ransom for their idolatry.

They have departed from the house of The Lord; they walk in the way of the infidel; they sit in the seat of the scorner; they are war-mongers and whores.

I say unto them, they are "whores" for they create like unto "THE WHORE". They are as the cast out, for they enter not into Mine house until they have purged themself, atoned for all their misused energy.

I say: "They shall atone for all their misused energy," and they shall enter into the Holy of Holies clean, and as the Sons of God - without spot or blemish.

Sananda

HE PREPARETH A TABLE BEFORE ME IN THE PRESENCE OF MINE ENEMIES

Be ye as one responsible for that which ye do with this Mine word; and ye shall add naught, neither shall ye take away aught. And bear ye in mind that I am He which hast given unto thee this part; and it is not of thine, yet, the responsibility of Mine Gift shall weigh heavily upon thine shoulders.

While I say I shall give unto thee all that ye can bear, I say I shall give unto thee no more.

And for that matter I shall deal justly with all men in all situations, and at no time shall I betray mineself or Mine trust. I say, I am The Lord thy God; sent am I. I speak unto thee with authority and Love, and no man hath greater Love than I.

I speak fearlessly and forthright, for I know well Mine subject. I fear no man's opinion, neither do I ask any favor - I am sufficient unto Mine part. I am of Mine Father sent; and with the authority which He hast invested in Me, I say unto thee, I am the Lord God and it is so. Let them which deny me or Mine authority come forth and prove themself, and I shall hear them out. And I shall be no less for their speaking, for I say there shall be much speaking; much murmuring and commotion. Yet, it is well that they speak of these things which I say, for in so doing they shall be as the wanton still; yet, the foolish shall be the foolish still, and there shall be no light amongst them save the truth of Mine Word. For their opinions and rantings shall in no wise change Mine Word, neither cast a shadow upon Mine Work - for them which heareth what I have said shall in no wise be moved by their rantings - their ravings.

Let it be given unto thee to see them for that which they are, and know ye that I am not of a mind to feed the dogs. Yet I say unto thee: "Come dine and be ye favored of Me, and I shall give unto thee food ye know not of." I say ye shall dine of honey/nectar from the choicest of the lilies, and that which I give unto thee shall be as the nectar which flows from Mine Chalice. I say, sup with Me and be ye as one refreshed, nourished, and we shall have Holy Communion - and it shall be a glad day.

For this is the day of The Lord. It is come - it is COME! Holy - Holy is the day of The Lord.

Be ye as one blest to receive Me and of Me.

Sananda

JUSTICE

Justice shall be Mine theme this day; and Justice shall reign, and no man shall be excluded or favored.

For I say, I am the one sent that the law of Justice be fulfilled. So be it that I am The Lord God sent of Mine Father.

For this am I prepared to deal out Justice unto all men, for it is in accordance with the Law that I give unto them as they are prepared to receive.

So be it that they which are prepared shall receive in greater measure; these shall have the greater meat - that which they are able to assimilate. So be it I shall give unto them as want to supply their need.

Be ye as one prepared to receive the greater part. Yet it is said, give not of thine meat unto the babes which have no teeth.

Let Me proceed with Mine subject of Justice. When one submits his will as a wholly/Holy sacrifice unto Me, he rebels not against the plan. He asks naught for self; he accepts gladly his part and fears not that he hast been forgotten. He swears no allegiance unto any man; he holds himself ready to serve in any capacity and at any time or place. He questions not his part; he fears not for his part - he accepts it with a glad heart. He stands at command, doing that which is to be done, and he feigns not wisdom, for he knows himself to be as a servant - and for, this he serves with humility and a glad heart. He sees the need and responds with a joyful heart.

Let it be said, his reward is the joy of serving. Yet he shall at all times remember that which is written, and he shall not fall into lethargy, for his laurels shall avail him naught should he fall into the pit.

I say the pitfalls are many, and I have pointed them out and marked them well. So be it that there are many milestones, and I say the last mile is the most treacherous, for the wind blows and the way is steep and narrow. I say watch lest thine foot slip.

Praise ye the Name of Our Father Solen Aum Solen; give unto Him thineself in Holy submission and confess thine weakness before Him. And ask of no man his blessing, for The Father of all knows thine need - for this hast He sent Me. So be it I come wielding the sword of Truth and Justice; and for this have | warned the candidate: "Be ye aware of the pitfalls," for it is Mine duty to forewarn them.

I come unto thee with great Love and compassion, for I see them as ones confused, confounded, rebellious, and starving for bread - Mine bread. While the rebellious refuse it, I say the ones which are seeking of Me shall take it, eat of it, and be nourished. Unto them I shall add to, and these shall be as ones prepared for the great feast which I shall prepare for them.

The call hast gone out: "Come ye unto the Feast," and I see them come! For they shall come, and they shall be glad.

See them come and be ye as one of them, and thine heart shall rejoice forevermore.

Sananda

FOR GENERATIONS TO COME

By Mine Works shall ye be set apart, for by Mine works shall ye be known to be of Me. And ye shall be as one humble of heart and a willing servant; and ye shall do that which I give unto thee, and at no time shall ye rebel against Me.

Now ye shall find thine hour hast come and Mine hand shall be upon thee, and ye shall be as Mine hand made manifest unto them. And at no time shall ye be as one in want, for I shall supply all thine needs, and ye shall be as one which hast been rewarded for work well done.

For this is Mine Word to be made available unto the ones which ask of Me; and I shall remember them even before they have asked - yea, even before they are born. For this Mine Work shall not end with this generation; nay, not with many generations, for I say Mine Works shall not pass away; they shall endure unto the end. So be it this is just the beginning of the new dawn, and much is yet to be accomplished before noonday.

Let it be said now that the new day shall bring with the next hour many changes, great changes, and they shall be good. The old shall be taken away, and the new shall be as the strength of many waters. And the day shall move with great rapidity, and time shall be as naught, for the onrush of mighty waters shall be manifestation of "The Word" which hast gone out; and it shall come upon thee swiftly and with great Light, for it shall be as the fulfilling of the Covenant made so long ago. I am come that it be fulfilled, so let it suffice that I am come - that I am The Lord thy God.

I say unto thee: There shall be an influx of power which man hast not known before, and he shall not endure it - which is not of the Light.

While it shall be understood that there shall be many taken from the dense body by natural cause; many shall be taken by violence; many shall be taken by means they know not of. And they shall be considered ill of mind, demented or insane, when they speak of the things which the world knows not of. Yet there shall be ones prepared for these things, for they shall be as the ones chosen to bear witness of these things which shall be new unto thee. These shall be as ones which shall be persecuted and pursued by the ones which think themself wise. Yet they shall be as ones rewarded, for they shall bear witness of that which I shall do; and they shall find their reward to be in the knowing; they shall be as the Knowers, and no man shall make of them fools, for I say I shall sustain them in the time of pursual and persecution.

Hear ye and remember Mine Words, for they are prophetic; and they shall come to pass, for I speak - I know whereof I speak, for I see it as done.

Yet they which labor for bread shall be within their places of labor, and they shall be no more there; they shall be no more here; they shall be as ones removed from among the others; without sign or sound shall they go. They shall be taken, and they shall not return unto their labors, for they shall not labor more for bread; neither taxes. Neither the foot nor the hand shall be weary, for they shall have rest. 1 say I have greater work for them.

Sananda

THIS I FIND

Say unto them as I would say, and in Mine name ye shall say these things, for it shall be for the good of all that I give unto thee these sayings.

They shall come unto me as willing servants - as ones willing to do the things I give unto them to do; and none shall have any opinions or preconceived ideas of that which I shall give unto them, for they know not unless I reveal unto them Mine Work aforehand.

As it hast been said many times: "As he is prepared so shall he receive."

Now it is Mine mission to prepare each and every one which is prepared to receive Me and of Me.

Ye ask: Are all not prepared for to receive thee? I say unto thee, nay! For they for the most part, are filled with self concern, self pity, self love, self gain, self importance - that they have no time for me. They hear not Mine words of admonition, neither preachments - Mine pleadings. Mine words they have denied; Mine servants they deny; they have closed me out of their houses of worship; they worship images - they know Me not! Yet I stand ready to give of Mineself that they might be lifted up. So be it that they which hear Me shall obey Mine commandments, and they shall be as the ones prepared, for I cannot use an unfaithful servant - one which hast betrayed himself or his trust.

Let it be written that he which betrays himself also betrays Me, for have I not entrusted into his keeping Mine place which is reserved for Me? For from the beginning a place was set aside for Me, where I might come and abide with each and every living soul. I say they have turned Me out, and the house of the Lord is filled with all sorts of iniquity and fornication.

I stand as a living witness of Mine Father which hast sent Me; I come in His name; I find them dead on their feet; the stench is such as no man can stand which hast once tasted of Living Waters - the Waters of Life. This is the Cup I bring. While they but make a mockery of Mine sayings and ridicule Me, I say I am come that there be Light - and the Light shall consume the darkness.

While it is but the beginning of this portion of Mine Work unto them, it shall be likened unto that which hast been said many times, for them which are yet to come - them which sleepeth still.

There are none so foolish as the one which thinks himself wise - none so sad as the one which betrays himself or his trust.

Now I shall add, that he which sets himself up and speaks words of wisdom in his own name, is like unto the child which babbles that which he hears and knows not the meaning thereof.

Let them first apply the word unto themself, then they shall know the value of that word; for if it be of no value unto him, why pass it unto another!

Fortune unto thine own self the meaning of Mine sayings, and it shall profit thee much.

Sananda

THE FALL OF THE NATIONS

Say unto them that they which are of Me abideth within the Light; that they which hear mine Voice and respond unto it shall find peace.

Yet, them which heareth Mine Voice and respond not, shall find no peace, for no place is peace to be found save in the Light which I AM.

Let it be said that I AM the Light; I AM THE WAY, and anyone whosoever walketh in The Way shall find peace.

They shall find safety, for I shall be their Shield and their Buckler; for I am The Lord thy God, and I have gone before them that the way be prepared before them, and I know every step of the way.

I come with the rod of Truth which is as a two-edged sword; it shall cut away all the untrue - all that which hast held bound Mine people. I say it shall cut clean and set Mine people free, for no longer shall an oppressed people suffer the indignities of an oppressor!

I say the oppressor shall be as the head of the serpent bruised with many bruises; he shall be as the serpent still, yet his head shall be bruised with many wounds; and they shall number 666, and there shall be no balm for his wounds. While it is given unto the serpent to be the serpent still, he shall be disarmed, for I say: A Mighty Host shall come forth to put him asunder. He shall be seen for that which he is, and he shall fall by his own weight, and a mighty crash shall it be, for with him shall go many nations; many which have set their temples up unto him and called him "God".

I say they shall fall with him! For they have paid homage unto him, and they have set him up as their God.

Now it is plainly written that no man shall pass within the portal - within the Holy of Holies unknown unto Me; and I say I know him not, for he is not of Me; he, the beast, is not of Mine house!

While he does call himself god, he has the mind to make subject Mine people. Yet I swear unto him, that he shall fall! For there is no truth within him; he is the father of lies and the mother of deceit!

Let thine time be spent in well-doing, and he shall have no power over thee, for he is the black magician and the father of illusion. Now I shall let this suffice for this - and ye shall be as ones alert, for he hast many fingers - and they are in thine own pocket! They pilfer the till of every honest man which labors for his bread.

Be ye as one forewarned, and seek ye thine own freedom as one prepared. Look for the Light; seek the Light; seek thine own salvation in the Light. Ask of no man for the Light, for no man can sell or bring salvation.

I ask of thee naught save obedience unto the Light - the Law, and ye have nothing to fear, for I say unto thee, Justice prevails.

Sananda

ACCORDING TO PLAN

Be ye as one prepared for that which ye shall receive within this part, for it shall be as a part separate from the other parts which have gone before this one. Yet, this shall be added unto the other parts which are now prepared.

One shall stand within thine midst as a bright and glorious light, and he shall be unto thee great assistance; and he shall be as one sent, for I shall send him. And he shall do a mighty work with thee, for he shall fulfill his mission, then he shall go as he came - so be it according to the plan.

The plan shall likewise be completed, and then there shall be greater parts to be put together; and the parts shall be as one whole when the great plan is revealed - and revealed it shall be.

Let it be recorded this day that the ones which come over this threshold shall be as ones blest; even there be traitors amongst them, they too, shall awaken, and they too shall see even as Paul, that they are not so wise. They too shall be as Paul - they shall be given as they are prepared to receive. So be it that I know their capacity - so shall that capacity be filled. I am one prepared to fill that capacity.

It is said: "I shall send one." So be it that he shall walk even as the one in flesh; yet he shall be more than flesh, for he shall be of Mine house. He shall be as the master, for he shall come with authority and power; he shall bring with him his credentials, and he shall also bear upon his forehead Mine Seal; and it shall be broken and ye shall read, and ye shall know - for this shall I send him. So be it that he shall come bearing a gift, and ye shall know him by his gift, for it shall be unto thee a sign, for I shall reveal unto thee the nature of that gift. Let it be for thee; accept it in Mine Name, for I have placed it within his hands that he might have the privilege of giving it unto thee. And after thou hast received it from him, thou shall give it unto Me, for it is Mine to give and to take, for this is it given unto him - so let it be as The Father wills it.

I am the Lord thy God, giver of all precious gifts. In mine Father's Name I pass the Cup unto thee; I say, drink ye deeply and be ye as one prepared to dwell in the house of the Lord forever. So be it I pronounce thee Mine hand-maiden which I have called out and chosen for this work - so be it I give unto thee Mine benediction.

O Most Holy and Blessed Father: I ask for this Mine beloved Hand-maiden which hast served Me well, that she now rest in the knowing that she is one with Me; that she is secure within Thine embrace; that Thine Will shall be her will, and that all which comes within her presence be blest of thee - even as Thou hast blest Me. O Father, I ask this in Thine Name that all be blest for the Glory and the Honor of Thine Own Blessed Being. I ask it that Thou be Glorified thru this Mine beloved.

Sananda

SONS OF GOD ARE MANY

Say unto them in Mine Name that the time is come when they shall forsake the way of the world, and they shall turn from the way of the foolish and be as ones sober and thotful. And they shall no longer be as the ones which have "The Book" in one hand and the other hand in the till. They shall be as ones responsible for that which they teach - that which they expound with such fervor!

I say, they shall be as ones prepared for that which they have set into motion, for surely it shall return unto them; it shall return bearing its likeness a thousand times multiplied!

While I say unto them: They shall put aside all their hypocrisy, and they shall stand naked before Me, the Lord God, and they shall be seen for that which they are - and they shall not deceive Me. It shall be given unto Me to know them for that which they are.

Now ye shall say: Are we not all Sons of God? I say unto thee, yea - yet I say, "Awaken ye Sons of God which sleepeth! For long hast thou slept.". This is the day of awakening, and I am come that it be so. Let it be known that I am come; that I am within the place wherein I am prepared to reveal Mineself unto any man which is prepared to receive Me!

Yet I say, I reveal Mineself not unto the profane and the unjust - I am not so foolish!

I give of Mineself that they might be prepared, yet they stir not; yet unto them which doth hear Mine Voice and respond unto it, I shall reveal Mineself. Yea, I shall touch them and they shall be quickened, and they shall know Me.

Hast thou given unto Me credit for being He which is The Lord of Lords, The Kings of Kings, The Host of Hosts? Hast thou given unto Me thine alms, thine sacrifice? I say unto thee, these things I ask not of thee - I ask of thee obedience unto the law. Be ye as ones respectful of the law, and I shall take note of thee. I shall give unto thee, and no man shall be unto thee as the oppressor, as the father, as the high priest. I am the High Priest, for Mine Father has given unto Me the authority to say that which I say, and no man has the same authority as He has given unto Me; for HE hast placed ME at the Door of the Inner Temple wherein HE abides, and none pass save thru Me.

This is Mine part, Mine place, Mine station, and I betray not Mineself, neither Mine trust.

Let it be understood that there are many Sons of God - I bear witness of them, and I speak now for them; and they stand at the right hand of God as witness of Me. And I proclaim unto thee, these Mine Holy Brothers are as ones in high esteem of Mine Father, for He hast given unto them their inheritance in full, and no man shall deprive them of it, for it is their eternal and divine estate which shall pass not away.

Blest are they, and blest are they which shall awaken unto their true identity - so be it I come that they awaken.

Sananda

24

SPIRIT IS FLUID

Say unto them in Mine Name that I come declaring Truth and Justice - this is Mine part, this is Mine time, and I shall go forth as a Mighty Army arrayed in Light - as arrayed in snow-white garments. For I shall bring with Me a Mighty Host, and they shall be as one body, one man, for they have but one purpose, one thot - that of our Father's Will; and it shall be done in us, thru us, and by us.

And no man shall stay the hand of God, for it shall move with surety and swiftness; it shall remove from the lands of the Earth the dross; it shall move before it the debris. And it shall be as a mighty and powerful Light, and nothing which is of evil shall stand before it.

Nothing which is of the darkness shall stand before it, for the darkness shall be dispelled by the Light, and nothing of darkness shall remain. The noon-day shall be at hand; then the cry of joy shall go out as of ten thousand harps within the hands of ten thousand angels, and the firmaments shall rejoice and be glad. So be it that this is the time spoken of long ago: "And the gates of heaven shall open up to reveal the Glory thereof."

Now upon that day all which now labor within the limitation of flesh - and for the good of all, and for the glory of The Father, shall be as ones brot forth in great glory; they shall have received their Royal Raiment and their inheritance. And they too, shall be as the Host, for they shall be as the awakened; they shall be as ones which have heard the call of the Mighty Host: "Awaken! All ye that sleepeth - Awaken! Awaken! All ye that sleepeth!"

And they shall rejoice and be glad, and no more shall they go into bondage - the bondage of flesh - for they shall stand free, even as I am free. And no more shall they sorrow; no more longing shall they know, for their longing shall be satisfied.

These shall be free, forever free! And no man knows such freedom while in flesh. I say unto thee. "Flesh is flesh! And comes under the law of flesh." I speak unto thee of Spirit! SPIRIT I say! And Spirit is not limited! I say Spirit is not limited; it is fluid and cannot be bound or housed in flesh or any other substance. It is a substance apart; a substance no man can analyze/place in a test tube/under a microscope/touch/see or give/or take. He is Spirit - he knows not that which he is; he knows not that he is eternal; he knows not that he is ONE with ALL; he hast not learned the "First lesson", for he thinks himself a thing apart - a creature of destiny upon the sea of matter; cut loose without a captain, without rudder or sail. He thinks himself sufficient unto himself. Yet how foolish, O man! For thou art more than flesh. Thou art eternal. say, ARISE! And claim thine Divinity, thine Sonship.

Let the Light be thine; let the Light which is MINE shine forth- be ye one with IT. Walk ye knowingly; see the Light and walk ye in IT; bear ye witness of Me and ye shall fail not, neither shall ye fall by the way. I say COME! Follow ye Me, and I shall lead thee into the path of righteousness which leads unto eternal freedom.

So be it. I AM The Lord thy God.

Sananda

26

I AM COME

Wait upon Me the Lord thy God and stand ye at command, for I shall command of thee obedience. And ye shall be as one responsible for thine ownself - and at no time shall ye be unto another responsible for his part, for 1 shall take command, and I shall be responsible for the command which I give.

Now I say unto each and every man: Thou alone shall atone for all the misused energy, the energy thou hast misused, and that is the law; there are none which escape the law.

While it is said ye alone shall atone for thine deeds and thine own misused energy; I, too, say, that there are ones to assist thee when thou hast stopt, looked, listened, and when thou hast heard that which I say.

I say unto each and every man which liveth: There is but the present, the eternal now. Listen unto Me, O ye men of Earth! And ye shall be blest to hear; for this have I spoken; for this I am speaking.

Let thine feet be swift to follow Me; let thine hands be swift to do Mine bidding; let thine tongue be swift to confess Me - to bear witness of Me. And at no time shall ye deny Me, for I say unto thee, pity is the one which denies the One Sent - and I AM HE! I AM HE!

Let it be known I am come - I AM COME. Lift up thine heart and rejoice that I am come, for this day shall ye come into the fullness of thine estate. I say: Them which follow Me shall rejoice with me that this day is come. Lift up thine hearts, O men of Earth; lift up thine eyes; see the hand of God move, and rejoice with Me.

For this is the day of the Lord; I say unto thee: "THIS IS THE DAY OF THE LORD THY GOD." Wait no longer, for I, have declared openly: "I AM COME - I AM COME!!"

There shall be great weeping and wailing - and great joy there shall be. There shall be a division, for the ones which have been as the traitors shall wail and weep, while the ones which follow Me shall know great joy, for they shall be delivered out of bondage, and they shall be forever free.

I am come with a Mighty Host, and the Host is equal unto Me, for they, too, are free; they, too, are ONE with Me, and I am One with Mine Father which has sent Me.

Now ye shall say unto them in Mine Name, that I come not to bring peace; I come that they might find Peace; that they might go where I go - and I go unto Mine Father which hast sent Me.

I bid thee Come; I ask of thee Come, enter into Mine place of abode and be ye at Peace - yet none enter unprepared.

I say, "Prepare thineself to enter in." I have given unto thee the Law; I have given of Mineself that the way be made clear before thee, and no man shall take from thee thine inheritance - yet thou shall prepare thineself for to receive it. By Mine Grace shall ye be prepared, for I am come that ye might be prepared. So let it profit thee to hear that which I say unto thee. I Am with thee -

I AM Sananda

THE ACCEPTABLE SACRIFICE

So it wast in the beginning - so shall it be in the end. Man hast given unto himself great sorrow and woe; he hast fortuned unto himself all his sorrow; now he shall know from whence it cometh.

He shall be given that which he hast stored up, for it is his, and no man shall deny him his fortune.

Yet I say, he shall weary of his own fortune and cry out for deliverance. He shall be as one delivered when he turns from it with a contrite heart and an humble spirit, for one shall be at his side to assist and direct him; to lead him into the way which leads to freedom.

I say, each man shall drink of the portion which he hast prepared. Therefore I say, prepare not the bitter cup, for ye shall drink every drop unto the last bitter drop.

Blest is the man which drinks of Mine Cup, for therein is no bitterness - no gall. No bitterness is contained within the cup which I proffer thee, for it is filled to overflowing with the Water of Eternal Life.

Be ye as one which can accept the Cup which I proffer thee; be ye as one blest to accept it for it shall be unto thee thine eternal freedom.

Hear ye Mine Words; accept them and be ye acceptable unto Me, and I shall say unto thee, pass ye into the Holy of Holies.

While I have said I give not of Mineself unto the filthy and unjust, I say, I give of Mineself unto all which seek Truth and Light.

I give of Mineself that ye might be brot out of darkness/ bondage - that ye might suffer no more.

I come that ye might know the true from the false - that ye might know the way unto Mine Father's House.

While I am the Wayshower, I am not of a mind to bring thee against thine own will.

I am not a tyrant or traitor. It is said that thine free will is the gift which thou wast endowed of by The Father, and He hast given it unto thee by His Own Will, and no man shall take it from thee, for it is thine by Divine Rite.

And when thou hast been as one prepared to surrender it up unto The Father which hast given it unto thee in the beginning, He shall accept it as thine passport into the Holy of Holies wherein He abides, for it shall be unto Him thy only sacrifice - the only sacrifice which He shall receive, for He accepts naught which He hast not given.

He, The Father, which hast sent Me, asks of thee: "Return unto me and I shall accept thee as a Son." Yet, He asks that ye be willing to return, and it is by thine own will that thou shall return.

Now let it be understood that the will is not the "Wish"; it is the action. It is ACTION, and it is that which thou become - thou shall not wish thineself free. Thine own puny will shall not free thee. It is said: Surrender up thine will unto The Father which has given it -

then He shall send one that shall lead and guide thee into His place of abode.

I am He which is sent, and I am The Lord of Lords, The Host of Hosts. I am He which sits at the Head of The Mighty Council, and I am prepared to be unto thee thine Counselor and thine Director.

So be it.

I AM Sananda

YE SHALL THEN SAY: YEA LORD

Say unto them that no man hast greater Love than I. I know their sorrow, their weakness, and I, too, know their strength.

For this do I speak out this day - I am come that they be strengthened in their weak parts, that they overcome their weakness.

Now for that matter, I am their strength; I am their refuge, and I know the way unto Mine Father's House. The way is strait and narrow, and I bid thee come with Me and I shall lead thee.

I come not bearing greetings and giving lengthy sermons of flowery words; I come simply without pomp or fanfare. I give no sign, neither do I give unto them miracles that they bow down and worship Me.

I give unto them the law, and I point the way and say, "Walk ye therein." And it is Mine part to be the "Wayshower", and at no time shall I mislead thee.

Time is no more; time is past when they which ask that I bear Mine wounds unto them that they might be satisfied. I say, no more shall they put their fingers into Mine wounds - they shall believe without seeing.

I say, blest is he which believeth while walking blindly - I say blest is he.

Now it is come when great stress shall be upon the peoples of all nations, and they shall cry out, and I say unto them, "This thou hast created." While I have cried from the mountain top, "Turn from thine own way; come up hither and I shall give unto thee peace."

Yet they go headlong, headstrong, into the fury of the battle - and battle there shall be; protest not! For they shall reap the harvest thereof. I say they have sown unto the wind; now they shall reap the tornado which they have brot about - so be it the LAW!

I say, the first law is: LOVE YE ONE ANOTHER! And have they Obeyed? I say they have not opened up their hearts unto Me. I ask of them, "Lovest thou Me?" I hear them answer, "Yea, Lord," and I say unto them: Ye are liars! For how comes it thou loveth Me and hateth thine brother? It is not so that thou LOVETH ME and hateth thine brother!

I say: Love thine brother as thine own self, and ye shall then say, "Yea, Lord."

While it is given unto thee to sell thine brother into bondage, I say unto thee: First, go cleanse thine heart of all its hatred - of all its impurities, iniquities, envy and malice, self-conceit. Then say unto Me, "Yea, Lord."

Now ye shall consider well thine own shortcomings first, then ye shall point thine finger at thine own self, and first remove the beam from thine own eye - then ye might see Me as I am. And to see Me is to know Me; to know Me is to LOVE ME as thou lovest Mine sayings. When thou hast understood Mine sayings, then ye shall love thine brother as thineself; and then ye can say "Yea, Lord, I lovest Thee" - and I shall take heed of thee.

Yet remember well, I am not deceived by thine honeyed words of flowery speech, I know that which prompts them.

Be ye as ones true unto thine own self and ye shall be as one made glad. Be ye blest of Me, for I come that ye be blest.

So be it The Father's Will.

Sananda

THE GOLDEN KEY

Be ye as one responsible for that which ye do, for thou art responsible unto Me for that which ye do. Thou art responsible unto thineself, and no man shall turn thee out, for I say unto thee there is but one way unto Mine Father's House - that I AM. I AM the door. I AM the Way.

I Am the Will of Mine Father which hast sent Me.

So be it I bid thee come and partake of Mine Cup; 1 bid thee drink of the water of Life, for this is the water of Eternal Life which I proffer thee. Shall it profit a man to gain the whole world, and lose his divine inheritance?

I have given unto thee much; yet thine eyes hast not beheld the Glory of The Lord; for I say, thine mortal eyes could not behold it - it is beyond man of flesh. That he could look upon such Glory would be Mine desire, then he could faintly know that which I know.

I speak in terms comparable unto the understanding of man; yet, he hast no comprehension of that which I say, for that which I must use from necessity - to convey Mine "Word" is so limited - for no language known to man of Earth can convey the great and glorious joy of the Eternal Verities, the Eternal Freedom, Eternal Bliss of which I speak.

To Know is Wisdom
To Know is to Be
To Be is to know

For this have I given unto thee The Covenant; for this have I covenanted with thee long ago.

I am now come that it be fulfilled - so let it be as The Father hast Willed it.

Now I shall speak of the words of the Spirits which keep watch. I say unto thee, the guardian Spirit walketh by thy side day and nite; and it is for this that thou art spared a fate worse than death, for there are none so low as to be deprived of a guardian Spirit.

While the Guardian has not the power of his own, neither the desire to trespass upon man's free will. I say unto thee, he is thine Benefactor; he is thine Brother unseen, which holds the lamp for thine feet so long as thou dost tread the way of flesh.

I tell thee of a surety: He is thine Benefactor which gives of himself that ye be sustained - the unswayed Benefactor.

He asks of thee naught save obedience unto the law. Man hast called this Spirit "Conscience", and by any other name he should be just as real, for he hast no name. He hast been forever Spirit, and by any name he exists - no less, no greater for the name given.

For no man knoweth the Love of God while he walks in flesh, for His Love and Mercy supercedes man's knowing. Yet I say unto thee, ye shall come to know, for this is thine divine right.

Call upon The Lord thy God and ye shall be heard, for I stand ready to assist thee - yet ye shall will it so. And for this I have given unto thee the "Golden Key" unto the Inner Temple wherein I abide.

Follow ye Me and I shall direct thee; do as ye will, yet I say come! And be ye forever free. I place within thine hand THE KEY - "Father, Thy Will be done in me, thru me, by me, and for me".

So let it BE.

Sananda

THE CLARION CALL

By Mine own Word shall they be brot to account, for i have given unto them the law; I have plainly said, they shall be responsible for that which they do with the WORD which I have given unto them. And when they see fit to spit upon it, they shall be brot to account for their foolishness, for it is given unto Me to see them as ones which think themself wise.

These are the fools! These are the ones which have their hands before their eyes - their fingers in their ears.

I say: Take thine fingers out of thine ears and hear Me, for it is now come when I shall send forth the word as a Mighty Trumpet, and it shall sound in all the lands of the Earth. And it shall be as the last trumpet, for this is the "Clarion Call". I say, no more shall I send forth Mine messengers, mine emissaries to be martyred by them, for it is now time that they awaken and come unto Me.

Wherein is it said that "never again shall I lower My Light that they be brot out of bondage." Now this day I say. "Come ye hither," and all which hear and come shall be brot out.

Let them which will come, and they shall find Peace. Let it be said that they which come unto Me shall go into bondage no more, for I am come that they be delivered forever.

Yet this is "The Day of Salvation", and this is the time for which ye have waited; this is the time foretold long ago - why wait longer?

Why waste thy substance?

Why lament thine lot when I proffer thee the Cup of Living Water? Why lament thine suffering, when I proffer thee rest?

Why pity thineself when I proffer thee perfect peace?

Why give unto thineself the bitter cup when I proffer unto thee the Cup which Mine Father hast provided thee?

Yet, I say ye shall accept it of thine own free will - I force naught upon thee. I bring the Sword of Truth and Justice, and I say unto thee, it is a two-edged sword - sharp, swift and clean; it is sure, and no man escapes the action thereof.

Let it be known that I am come that the law be fulfilled; that thou might be given the law. And it is given unto Me to know the action of the law, and no man disobeys it without consequence. I stand by as one with hands tied, and I am powerless to do Mine part, for there is a law preventing Me from doing that which is thine part.

Thine part is for thee, and thou alone art responsible for thine own preparation. I say: Prepare thineself for to receive Me and of Me, for I AM The Lord thy God. So be it I am come that ye might know Me; and for this have I called thee; for this have I said, "Come!" And when thou hast heard and answered, then I shall reveal unto thee many things which thou hast not yet dreamed of.

I say, thou knowest not Mine mind; Mine hand is not staid; Mine hand is swift to give unto thee as thou art prepared to receive. So let it profit thee to come and partake of Mine fortune - and be ye blest as I am blest of Mine Father - so let it be.

I AM Sananda

YEA, EVEN UNTO THE "DOG"

Say unto them that the whore is now to repent of her own misused energy, and she shall be as one forgiven; and new life shall be put into her, for she shall be as one resuscitated - recovered from her suicidal tendencies.

For, but by Mine Grace she should perish from the face of the Earth. Now ye, Mine beloved, shall give unto them that which I have shown unto thee in symbol. Ye shall not discount that which I give unto thee to see; and it is that which thou knowest, for it is in its purest form - that which I show thee; for it is wordless revelation and requires no media, for it is implanted upon thine heart - never to be erased.

Be ye as one prepared for the greater part, for I say unto thee: Great power shall be released, and ye shall have a greater part, and no man shall be unto thee a barrier. Let thine own feet be firmly planted upon the Rock which I AM, and I shall hold thee steadfast, and I shall be unto thee sufficient. Have I not given unto thee in great capacity, and have I not given unto thee in great strength?

Have I not said that the WORD is Power - Light? And have I not said that it shall go forth unto all the lands of the Earth for the good of all the world?

I say: It is now come when the whore shall repent, and she shall be resuscitated and she shall have a part; yet, i say she shall repent - and be resuscitated!

Lo - I see it as done!

Yet the dust shall remain. It, too, shall return unto dust, but MINE WORD shall remain - it shall not pass away.

For I, The Lord thy God, am the Author of Mine WORK, and no man shall hide it, and none shall keep it unto themself.

For I, The Lord thy God, speaketh with power and surety, authority, and I say unto thee: Place that which I have given unto thee before them, and it shall be given unto them without being edited or worked over by man, for I weary of them which set themself up as Mine critics, for they think themself wise.

I spew them out of Mine mouth, for I am capable of speaking in any manner which I see fit. I am not limited. I say unto thee: Man is the bigot, laboring under the limitation of flesh; he hast not the unlimited power which hast been given unto Me by Mine Father.

I say Mine Father has given unto Me Mine Divine Inheritance in full! And no man shall deprive Me of it, for no man hast that power.

So be it that I have shown unto thee many things; yet, it is not given unto thee to find language whereby they might be informed, or enlightened, or apprised.

Yet unto them which doth answer Mine call shall be given, even as I am given. I say unto all: COME! And unto them I say, it shall be given, yea, even unto the "Dog".

I am come that ALL might be saved.

Sananda

41

THE DEAD

By Mine hand they shall be resuscitated; by Mine Grace shall they be restored.

Now let us speak of the dead. These are ones which have no will; these are the ones which know not their Source, their origin. These are the ones which have not the will to return unto their Source. These are the ones which have fallen from their high estate. These are the ones which have come into flesh many, many, times knowing not that they are bound by flesh.

They know not that they have but to seek their freedom thru the Source of their being, and it shall be given unto them. It is said, "Seek ye the Light, and it shall not be denied thee."

For this is it said, "As ye seek, so shall ye find." They which seek their fortune within flesh shall find; yet, I ask of them: Wherein hast it been given unto thee to find freedom? Wherein hast it been given unto thee to find Peace? Wherein hast it been given unto thee to know thine Source?

For there are but few which know by which they are bound.

I say: They are the ones which are dear; and the second death is that which follows the first; and is it any better that a man dieth twice?

While it is said, the second death is the beginning of the awakening, I say it is the beginning of the end. So let him awaken from the dead and be as one come alive!

For this is it said, "Awaken all ye that sleepeth!"

Where is there a man which knoweth the power of The Word? I say, bring him hither, and I shall show thee wonders which ye know not of!

Behold the power of The Word, and be ye made new!

I say: Behold the power of The Word and be ye made new. So be it I shall speak the Word which shall bring new Life into the old - and the old shall pass away, and all things shall become new.

So be it I have spoken the Word, and it shall take form and be manifest in form, and ye shall behold it and be glad, for I say even thine eyes shall behold the new. And the passing of the old shall bring much joy, and likewise great sorrow unto the ones bound by flesh, for they shall behold their flesh as torn and rent. They shall see their blood spilled, and they shall cry out, "Lo, we perish!"

I say unto them: Thou hast worshipped flesh! Thou hast lived by flesh - now thou perish in flesh.

So let it be, for I have called out in Mine longing for thee - the fallen one Israel: "COME!" Yet thou hast waited overtime; now ye perish of thine own sluggishness. So be it the Law.

I say unto thee: Hear Me this day! Pick up thine feet; come hither and abide ye by Mine Words; follow ye Me and I shall lead thee out of bondage. I am the One Sent, and thou hast not given unto Me credit for being that which I AM. The Lord thy God

Sananda

43

THE SACRIFICE

Say unto them that by their faith they shall come to know that which I say unto them to be of The Father, for their faith in Me shall be justified. And by their faith they shall seek Me, and I shall not give unto them a stone, neither shall I give unto them more than they can bear.

While it is said that even the bread of the children have to be broken for them. It is so, for they are not as yet prepared to partake of the food from Mine board; neither shall they drink of the Water of Life until they have first had the smaller portions, for they could not assimilate it.

There are ones which are now prepared for the greater portion - yet, they wait. It is oft-times necessary that they wait, for there are times when this is the greater reward,

So be it that this waiting is the greater joy, for when it is finished - and the work seen as finished - it shall bring greater joy and peace unto the one which hast given himself in such self-sacrifice. This is the selfless work, the sacrifice that is acceptable unto Me.

It is said: Be ye as the servant of The Lord thy God; bring thyself as a living sacrifice, for none other can He use. It is said that as a man prepareth himself so shall he become. It is the law; and for this is it said, "Prepare thineself for to receive Me and of Me," for none other shall I receive unto Mineself.

Wherein is it said, "I am the Doorkeeper and none pass save thru Me - they deceive Me not!"

Let them be prepared, for this have I sent Mine Messengers, Mine Servants, Mine Emissaries unto them in untold numbers; and these have for the most part been rejected by the world.

I say unto them, O men of the Earth, bear ye in mind thou art not alone; thou art not alone!

For thou art a boastful, lustful, bigoted, ignorant lot, and it is the pity of thine plight!

While there are worlds untold that thou knowest not of; and there are things which ye have not seen, lessons yet unlearned, and worlds beyond thine grandest hopes or imagines - yet thou fain wisdom. Oh, ye sucklings! Bear in mind, "There are none so foolish as the ones which think themself wise!"

Wherein is it said that the way into Mine Father's House is strait and narrow. It is so. And let it be understood that I am the Way; I come that ye enter in; yet ye shall obey the law which is placed before thee, and none pass unnoticed, none pass thru unprepared.

Let it be said, I have prepared the Way; now I come saying unto thee, "Walk ye in the Way, for I am The Light, The Truth, and The Way". So shall it ever be, for I am He which IS SENT of Mine Father; I am sent that I might find them which are prepared to receive Me.

This is the day of The Lord, and I say unto thee: Prepare thineself for to receive Me and of Me, then I shall bid thee enter into Mine place of abode. I shall say unto thee, "Pass ye in," and ye shall be glad for thine preparation. And ye shall partake of Mine board, and all thine hunger shall be satisfied, and ye shall know no more longing, no more sorrow, no more suffering. Then ye shall receive thine reward for service well done, and I shall say unto thee, "Abide with Me forever".

Sananda

THE ACCOUNTING

Behold in Me the Light which I AM; consider well thine own Light, thine Source. Ponder the sayings given unto thee; ponder thine own sayings, compare them, and know ye that which prompts them. For I, The Lord thy God, knoweth thine every intention, thine every need, and I am not want to leave thee in darkness. I say unto thee: Be ye as one prepared to receive Me and of Me, and be ye as one blest.

Now let us consider well the time. The time is come when great Light shall go forth from the Mighty Council, and it shall flood the Earth, and all shall feel the power thereof. Yet not all shall stand before it; not all shall endure it, for they resist the Light - and of these I say, they shall perish.

Now let it be understood that to lay aside thine earthly garment of flesh is not to perish, for the garment of flesh is but the earthly vehicle, and it is a fragile and clumsy thing. While it is said flesh binds thee, it is also said that Spirit is not bound by flesh. And, too, it is said, that Spirit is fluid, penetrating all living things; it is for the Spirit that it liveth, for were it not for Spirit there would be no animation of the world of matter. For that matter, it is Spirit which animates the inanimate form, as well as, the animated which thou knowest. I say, it is for the Spirit that ye live and breathe. So be it that there is Light within the breath; and as for the breath, did not The Father breathe into man's nostrils the Breath of Life - thus he became a Living Soul or Spirit? While it is said, no man can give Life or take away; it is said, he can deprive a Spirit its vehicle. And it is said, it is better to lose thine own than to destroy that of another; yet, have they taken heed of these things?

I say, nay! They have not! I say, pity are the ones which deprive another his vehicle, for it is as his possession - as his - and no man hast the right to deprive him of it; for he hast gathered about him the substance of flesh, and The Father hast animated it with Life. So be it man is co-creator with The Father, and for this I say unto man: Destroy not the house of The Lord - the tabernacle of God! For He, The Father which hast sent Me, hast willed unto thee so many days upon the Earth, and no man shall trespass upon the Holy Ground without suffering the consequence. It is said, woe unto any man which deprives another of his right of expression in physical form - so be it the law.

Hear Me, O ye men of Earth! Hear ye Me! I say unto thee: Lay aside thine instruments of death and turn unto the Light. See the Light and walk ye in it, and be as one forever free.

I speak unto thee, o man that ye might be prepared, for the day draws nigh when ye shall be brot to account, and ye shall face thine own self in the accounting. And ye shall remember Mine Words, and bitter shall be the cup which thou has prepared for thineself. I bid thee Come, forsake thine ways, drink of Mine Cup, and ye shall find Peace.

Sananda

THE NEW DISPENSATION

Say unto them, that while it is now come that there is a new dispensation, and a part for each and every one, it behooves them to make ready themself to be as ones prepared that they might join with the Great and Mighty Host which stands by at this time.

I say, the Mighty Host now stands ready to give unto each and every one a part. And it is given unto Me to see them at their labors wherein they labor for bread - as ones bowed down, oppressed, knowing not that there is relief.

They ask of their fellow men relief; they ask of their oppressors relief; what have they found? Their oppressors are likewise oppressed, for I say unto them: The oppression is not confined unto the ones in the flesh; it is not originated in the flesh only, for there is a force which hast gone forth for generation after generation, yea, hundreds of generations, and it hast collected itself together as one mighty body. Now the force is called the "dark force"; it is an intelligent force, yet, it is not of the light. It is of the dark.

For this is there "War in Heaven"; for this does the Sons of God draw nigh, that the people of the Earth might not be swallowed up; that they might be brot out.

Now let it be understood that the dark forces are manipulated - they are manipulated by the oppressors, for the oppressors serve the forces of darkness. And this force is implemented by man's misuse of the power, the "Power of God," which is his from the beginning.

And it is man's great and Divine right to know wherein he is bound - by which he is bound.

It is his Divine Inheritance to know that which is his freedom, by which he is freed from bondage. Therefore, I say: Look, listen, see that which goes on about thee; and hear ye that which I say unto thee, for I am the Lord thy God sent of Mine Father that ye might not perish.

I say unto thee this day: Ye shall first accept Mine Word, Mine servant, then I shall take note of thee. I shall touch thee, and I shall lead thee all the way.

It is said, "As thou art prepared so shall ye receive," it is the law - ye shall abide thereby. And think ye not to deceive Me, for I see and know that which thou art; think ye not to set Me in a corner, for I shall be put into a corner no more.

I am come that ye might have Light; and when ye deny Me, ye deny Mine Father which hast sent Me; when ye deny Mine servant, ye have denied Me.

I say unto thee, I have called this Mine Servant out from amongst them which serve the forces of darkness; and I have bestowed upon this one which I call Beloved, Mine blessings; I have set aside a part for her, and no man shall take from her one iota of her part, for I have given it unto her in the Name of Mine Father which hast given it unto Me.

Now for that matter, no man shall say that I am not of Mine Father sent, for it is not given unto them to know Me; and to know Me is to know The Father which hast sent Me.

I have first revealed unto this one so many years ago, the Name which I now bear; and to them which are of the Order of Melchezedek I say, This is Mine Name by which ye shall know Me, for this is the Order of Melchezedek, and I am He which hast opened up the Door in this day. At this hour I stand with sword in hand and I bid thee: Come; and I say unto all which hear Mine Voice: Ye shall be as ones protected; fear not, come ye hither and no harm shall befall thee, for I am the Door Keeper, and to all which are so prepared I say, "Pass ye in."

So be it I AM The Lord thy God

Sananda

TIME IS LIMITED

Say unto them, their time is limited; they know not the hour; it shall come when they have not the strength nor the time to cry out, for it shall be as nothing they have known; when a mighty sound shall ring out, and they shall be brot up short.

I say, they shall be caught up short of their course, and they shall cry without ears to hear; they shall cry out for the desolation and waste.

I say: Behold! Behold! Behold the desolation! For it has lain waste the land. Ye shall say unto them, "Behold!" And they shall be as ones sightless, for they shall have no eyes to see. I say unto thee: The desolation shall lay waste the land, and it shall be as thou hast not seen.

While it is said: This is Mine Land, Mine place, Mine fortress for many peoples; I say, Mine people have betrayed their trust; they have been untrue unto themself, they have forgotten from whence comest their rights, their inheritance. Yet, they know not that which they have forfeited, for they are as the foolish.

I say, foolish, indeed, are they, for they have set foot against Me; against Mine prophets. They have been given the Word; they know the law; yet, they have made a laughing subject of Me. The have ridiculed Mine Priests, Mine Emissaries; they have martyred Mine prophets in the name of their god!

I say: The Father hast sent me and they accept Me not!

While it is said, they which follow Me shall be brot out of bondage; yet, too, I say, bondage is of their own making; and they that are bound in Earth shall be bound in Heaven (wherein they shall find themself after they have lost their earthly garments), for they take with them their own fortune - that which they fortune unto themself.

I have said, "Cleanse thineself; cut away thine legirons and come unto Me, and I shall touch thee; I shall deliver thee up." Too, I say, thou are not sufficient unto thine own self. I say, "Thou art not sufficient unto thineself." For that hast Mine Father sent Me, and I shall come in and sup with thee, and ye shall be glad.

Harden not thine heart, O man of Earth, for I say unto thee, Thine heart shall be broken in twain ere I enter in, for it is given unto Me to see thee as one of hearts of stone; and it shall be cleft in twain, then I shall enter in - it is said thou hast turned Me out.

While I say unto thee, O man, ye shall no longer make a mockery of Mine Words; Mine servants shall stand exalted before thee, while thou shall stand in sack-cloth and ashes. Ye shall see thineself for the pity which thou art - dirty, filthy, ragged, yea, naked and hungry, while I shall prepare a table before Mine servants, and they shall drink from Mine Cup, and they shall prosper and be glad.

Yea, man of Earth, thou hast drunken of the blood of the Saints; thou hast devoured the husks from the swine's belly, and called upon thine servants to make music while thou hast played upon the five-stringed lute. I say, pity shall be thine plight. Give unto Me ear before the 12th hour strikes, for it draweth nigh when ye shall cry out for Mine assistance, and I shall hear ye from afar; for I am come this day that ye might have that which I bring unto thee - and ye shall accept it or reject it as thou will. Yet it shall not be said of Me that I wast asleep at the third watch.

I AM The Lord thy God

Sananda

HAST THINE WISDOM BEEN SUFFICIENT?

Say unto them: Wherein hast all thine wisdom availed thee aught, hast it earned for thee thine eternal freedom? Hast it earned for thee thine eternal freedom, I ask thee? I ask thee, "Hast all thine wisdom won for thee thine freedom?"

Hast all thine wisdom been unto thee. thine eternal salvation? Hast all thine wisdom been unto thee sufficient to deliver thineself out of bondage?

I say unto thee, O man of Earth, Thou hast not been unto thineself true; thou hast forfeited a princely fortune; thou hast denied thine inheritance; thou hast turned thine face from thine Source, and thou hast denied Me, The Lord thy God.

Thou hast wasted thine substance; thou hast flattered thineself, while thou rushed into destruction. I tell thee of a surety thou art not wise!

In no wise do I find one amongst thee that hast been sufficient unto himself.

For this hast the Host drawn nigh unto the Earth, and the Host sleeps not, for it is not given unto sleep, for sleep is no part of Them which make up The Host.

While thou dost for the most part deny The Host - and for that matter ye deny Me - I say unto thee, thine denial of Me shall be thine own downfall, for I AM THE ONE SENT that ye be lifted up.

55

Yet, ye shall reach out thine own hand that I might take it, for it is said: Ye shall come unto Me of thine own will, for none bring thee against thine will. None forch (sic) upon thee thine own part which is kept for thee - ye shall step forth and claim it, for it is thine by divine right.

Yet it is truly said, Ye shall prepare thineself for to receive it. "How do I prepare?" I hear thee ask. I have given thee the law; I have plainly stated the conditions upon which I have made Mine Covenant with thee.

I have waited; I have pleaded; I have coaxed and prayed with thee, O man of Earth! "Forsake thine way and COME UNTO ME, and I shall give unto thee as thou art prepared to receive."

Hear ye then that which I say unto thee, and I shall not mislead thee! I shall guide thee aright, and I shall prove Mineself. Yet it is said, "Blest is he which follow Me asking no proof," for they ask proof of Me! And they give unto Me none - none whatsoever!

I say: Give unto Me at least as much as thou asketh of Me.

I ask of thee naught save obedience unto the law.

Walk ye in the way I set before thee; prove thine worth and I shall not fail thee.

Walk ye humbly, and fear no man's opinion or opposition, for I am with thee unto the end.

How long shall I strive with thee, O man? I say, I shall strive with thee so long as thou art of a will to serve Me. I shall strive with thee so long as thou art worthy of Mine efforts. I shall strive with thee so long as thou dost make of thee a fit place for Mine abode. And when thou hast cleansed thine house, I shall enter therein, and I shall abide with thee, and ye shall sup with Me, and we shall rejoice together. Such is Mine Word unto thee this day.

So be it I AM The Lord thy God.

Peace - Peace - Peace

Sananda

ONE SOURCE OF LIGHT

Say unto them: There is but One Source of Light, and from IT cometh all Light, all Energy, all Revelation, all Intelligence - and from that Source, they have their Being.

For that Source is the Cause of Being, and for that thou hast the will - so lovingly endowed unto thee - O ye ungrateful men of Earth. I say unto thee, Thou hast not known such Love as The Father hast for His Children, O ungrateful children!

Knowest thou that He hast brot thee forth out of the fullness of His Love? And it is to thine own glorification that I ask of thee, Arise and come unto me that I might give unto thee as I have received of Him, Mine Father, that ye might return unto Him with Me.

For I tell thee of a surety, I shall go unto Mine father and I shall take with Me the ones which are so prepared. And they which have denied Me shall be left, and they shall be as the ones which have betrayed themself, and their cries shall avail them naught.

Say unto them which doth deny Mine Word, that they have not seen, neither heard, that which I shall do or say, for I am not finished - I AM NOT FINISHED! I am come that it BE finished; that it might be done - that which I have said I shall do.

For I am not of a mind to leave Mine part unfinished, for I have covenanted with Mine people long ago, and I say unto thee I am not a traitor, neither do I forget that which I have said.

I come that ye be prepared for thine part. Now let it be understood the Earth is the school-room, and thou shall prepare thineself therein for the next place - for therein is wisdom. And it shall stand thee foursquare to heed Mine Words, for I say the flesh shall perish, and the Spirit shall endure. So be it that Spirit is Eternal and everlasting, and it shall become thee to become as the Son of God; and ye shall wear the Royal Raiment, and ye shall stand spotless before Me. For this have I said, "Prepare thineself for the greater part."

And it shall be given unto thee to be as one which hast Mine hand upon thee and I shall say unto thee, Welcome! Enter ye into Mine place of abode and abide with Me, and we shall rejoice together.

Let it be understood that all thine world possessions shall be unto thee as naught; they shall no longer bind thee, for ye shall put them away as the chaff, and they shall have no charm for thee. Ye shall put them from thee! And ye shall have nothing which ye call "mine," "mine own," for it is said thou hast nothing except thine free will, which is thine only gift endowed unto thee - which is thine by Divine Right. Yet it shall be asked of thee: Surrender it up unto The Father which hast given it, for He is the Giver of all good Gifts - and unto Him all the Praise and the Glory Amen - so be it and Amen.

I, The Lord thy God, hast spoken this day.

Sananda

59

THE SWORD AND TRUMPET

Say unto them that I am The Lord thy God, and I forever shall be One with Mine Father which hast sent Me, for I am He which is sent that this day bear fruit.

While it is said that the day is but new, and the noonday is not yet come; it is said that it is the Day of Awakening - and it is for this that I come, that ye awaken from thine deep sleep.

Now it is said, thou hast slept overtime - it is so; for long have I cried, "Awaken! The time is come for thee to awaken!" Yet thou hast slept on.

Hear ye Me, for I say ye shall hear - for this I bring with Me a Great Host; I bring with Me a Mighty Sword, a Mighty Trumpet. The Sword shall be as the two-edged sword; the Trumpet shall be as nothing before heard by man, for it shall quake the Earth unto its very foundation, and all eyes shall turn unto the heavens; all knees shall bend; all tongues shall confess, and every heart shall be humbled. For I say, I shall sound the trumpet, and I shall wield the sword, for it shall cut away the effluvia, and the web of illusion which hast held fast them which profess Mine Name. It hast enmeshed them, and they know not the true from the false - they shall be glad for their freedom.

I say they shall rejoice for their new freedom, and it shall be cause for rejoicing, for long have they been caught up in the web.

I say: They shall be of a mind to follow Me; they shall be of a mind to go where I lead them; they shall be of a mind to accept ME for that which I am; they shall accept MINE WORD and Mine servants; they shall love one another and be at peace. I say, they shall be at peace, for I do not enter into the temple wherein confusion dwells, for confusion is no part of Me.

I say, "Prepare thineself for to receive Me and of Me," and then I shall come in and abide forever - so be it and Selah.

Be ye as one responsible unto Mine Voice, and be ye swift to do that which I give unto thee to do; and let thine tongue be swift to declare the Glory of God, for He dwelleth within all things which He hast made.

He abideth within all things which is created for His Glory. For His Glory wast thou brot forth, O man of Earth, and thou oweth thine first allegiance unto Him, thine Source. So let it profit thee to remember Him all the days of thine life. Glorify Him with the words of thy mouth; the work of thine hands; and let thine footsteps be onward and upward. Trip not! For it is now come when ye shall account for thine own self and all thine energy which is allotted unto thee.

Hear ye these Mine Words, and be ye as one blest; for this have I sent them forth; for thy sake have I spoken; for thy sake hast these Words been spoken and recorded. So be it. I shall prepare another part for thee - lay not aside this portion until thou hast perused My Word unto the end. So be it as The Father hast willed it, Amen and Selah. Mine Seal I have placed upon this Mine Priestess, and the Word is recorded in its perfection, and none shall say it is not of Me, The Lord which speaketh, for I have chosen well Mine Words, and

Mine servant hast been carefully prepared and selected - so let it suffice thee.

I AM HE which is sent of Mine Father this day.

So be it I AM Sananda

THE CUP OF LIVING WATER

Say unto them: The mighty and the haughty shall be brot low, while the humble and lowly shall be exalted. And they which set themself up shall be brot before the Elders and they shall be found wanting, for they shall see themself for that which they are.

They shall find themself unprepared, for they shall be as the "Foolish Virgins" - they shall find themself in darkness without oil.

I say they shall be found wanting; they shall find themself in darkness without oil.

Now to be without oil is to be found wanting; to be without oil is to be in darkness.

Yet I say unto them which ask of Me; it shall be supplied. So be it they shall seek the Light, and it shall not be hidden from them, neither shall they be caught up short, for they shall have their lamp trimmed and burning.

While it is said that many stand ready to give unto thee as thou art prepared to receive, it is also said, Empty out the old wine of great strength and I shall give thee Water more potent. So be it I am the One Sent that there be Light - so be it as The Father hast willed it. I proffer thee the Cup of Living Water; I ask of thee, "Drink and be ye made new; be ye made whole."

I bid thee, Drink! And be as one purified and made whole. This is Mine gift unto thee this day, for long have I awaited this day when

I might step forth and say unto thee, "Pass ye in" - and for this have I waited. I have waited long!

Now I bid thee, Come and partake of Mine Cup; drink and ye shall thirst no more. So be it that I am filled and I know no longing, for I am satisfied; and for this I know the satisfaction of the Cup I proffer thee, for I have drunken thereof and I say unto thee: It is sweet indeed. No bitterness shall ye find in Mine Cup, for I have put it to Mine lips and I know whereof I speak.

I say unto thee: I give unto thee as Mine Father hast given unto Me, and we shall be as the Sons of God which hast returned unto their rightful estate.

I speak unto all which hear Mine Words and obey Mine Voice; them which give unto Me credence for being that which I AM. And unto them I shall give Mine Peace, and I shall give unto them the Cup of Living Water - so be it is free for the taking - and it is given unto Me to know them which are prepared to receive.

So be it and Selah.

Sananda

I AM THE HOLY COMMUNION

Say unto them: They shall be as ones purified of all their hatred, their own willfulness, their own deceit, their own wanton, their hypocrisy, and so shall they be prepared to enter into Mine place of abode.

Then they shall be as ones free from all their preconceived ideas of Me and about Me, and they shall receive of Me; for then I shall hold out the hand which they are wont to refuse, afore their preparation. Because of their rebellion and wanton, have they refused - because of their conceit and foolishness.

Now I say unto them: They have but to rid themself of all their conceit, self-will, their hatred, malice and opinion, their greed, and then I shall give unto them of Mine portion.

Then, I shall give unto them the Bread of Life, and they shall know the meaning of "Holy Communion".

THEY HAVE NOT KNOWN

Yet it is given unto Mine servants to know, for I have given unto them the "Bread and Wine"; I have placed within their mouth Mine Word, and I have placed the Cup unto their lips and they have tasted thereof, and they have become sobered - for I have not given unto them that which should confuse them and make of them drunkards.

I say, they which make a mockery of the Holy Rites of the Sacrament are as foolish babes poll-parroting their rigmaroles; they know not the meaning of "Holy Communion". Yet they parrot their creeds: "I believe in Holy Communion, the communion of Saints" - yet, I ask of thee, O foolish mortals: Who are the Saints? Have you not martyred them because of their Holy Communion?

I ask thee, O ye foolish mortals: Have you had this Holy Communion? Knowest thou that it wast first by the Holy Communion that the Word wast made known unto thee?

Knowest thou that by the Holy Communion these Words are now being given unto thee. What sayest thou of this?

Knowest thou that Mine arm is long and strong, and I extend it unto all which art prepared to partake.

Yet let it be known that I give not unto the worshipers of IDOLS! I withdraw Mine hand from the hypocrite and the whoremongers.

I say, I am not so foolish as to waste Mine substance that they might boast of their power or position; that they might puff themself up and strut before men.

I come in simplicity; I give in simplicity, and I use no affluence to prove Mine worth. I give no proof unto the unbelievers, that they might believe - for they believe not THE WORD! Do they ask more?

I say, I bring the Word; the two-edged Sword; the Sword of Light!

And no man shall wrest it from Me, for 1 yield it not unto any man.

Let him that heareth come unto Me, and I shall touch him, and he shall know me, and he shall be glad for his knowing. So be it that I AM HE which hast been sent that all men be lifted up - wait thou for another?

I say: I AM HE WHICH IS COME.

Sananda

THE PLACE IS PREPARED

Say unto them that the place is prepared for them, and they shall be put into it, each according unto his preparation. And none shall be out of his proper place or environment, for each shall find his own environment and his own place.

None shall be put into another's place, for there is a place prepared for each and every one.

Now I say, according unto his preparation he shall be placed, for each shall qualify himself for his place. It is said: Cut away thine legirons, for none bring with them their possessions. It is said, thou hast nothing, not even the AIR thou dost breathe". Thine only gift that thou canst lay claim unto, is thine free will - and that is a gift of The Father which hast sent Me. This, too, shall be asked of thee.

I say unto thee: Lay not up store, for it shall be as trash - as the chaff blown by the wind.

Give unto Me credit for knowing that which I say unto thee, for I am not of a mind to mislead thee. I speak that ye might be prepared to go where I go - and I go unto Mine Father which hast sent Me.

Hear ye Me and I shall tell thee more, for think ye not that I have no more to say. Yet thou hast not heard that which I have said; and thou hast choked on the crumbs which I have fed thee, as the babe which hast not teeth for greater bread.

Be ye as ones which have ears to hear, and be ye as ones alert and stand at attention! For I shall call thee out from amongst them at the midnight hour, and ye shall arise and answer Me with these words: "Here am I, Lord! Here am I, Here am I". And I shall see thine Light and I shall know thee by it; and when it is sufficient I shall summon thee hither.

Let it be understood that the call shall be heard in all the lands of the Earth by all men; and they shall have no time to turn unto their fields; neither to return for friend or family, for it is said: Ye come hither - leaving ALL where they stand. Fear not, for I am the Lord thy God, and I am come that ye be led out of bondage. So let it be as thou hast willed it, for none bring thee against thine will.

So let it be said now, that I am come that each and every creature be lifted up. Yet, o man, why art thou so rebellious against Me, when I proffer unto thee thine freedom? Thou seekest freedom of men, O foolish man; 1 say they, too, are under the black hood; they knowest not freedom, it is not given unto them to be free. For what seekest thou? Seekest that which man hast and be ye cursed; seekest that which I have and be free.

I say unto thee: I am no respecter of persons; yet I know thine preparation; I give exactly as thou art prepared to receive - no more, no less. Yet I say, thine capacity shall be increased; for this have I said, prepare thineself to receive in greater measure.

I shall withhold naught from thee which thou canst bear, for I am come that ye be lifted up.

So let it be

Sananda

'TAPS' FOR THE DEAD

Say unto them: They shall find their reward in service rendered; in service unto mankind; in service unto the Great and Mighty Council. For it is by, and thru man that We work; it is thru obedience unto the LAW that thou art prepared to serve, for none other can serve US of The Mighty Council.

While We are at all times prepared to give counsel unto anyone, anywhere, at any time; 1 say that we do not counsel the hypocrite or the bigot, for he does not allow us to enter in - he turns a deaf ear, for he thinks himself sufficient, in his ignorance of us of The Council. He gives us no credence; he simply puts his fingers in his ears and says: I will not listen.

Be ye as one which has a mind to hear, for I say: The Word shall sound forth like a mighty trumpet - and yet it shall sound "Taps" for the dead - and it shall be as the death knell unto the dead, for the dead shall be like unto them which go into the second death.

These shall again be brot out of their place of abode and put into a place wherein they shall learn well the lessons they have refused to learn herein. This is the fortune of everyone which refuses to accept Mine Word this day; they shall wait long, for the place wherein they shall be put is in no wise a place in which they are forced to learn.

They wait, and wait again, until of their own volition they ask and desire Our help. Then We see that which they fortune unto themself; and when they are sufficiently prepared, We raise them, and we put them into yet another place wherein We might counsel them.

Yet, as they ask, so do they receive; as they fortune unto themself, so it is given.

Now let it be said: Let them seek the Light; seek the Way, The Truth, and it shall not be hidden from them.

When they seek phenomena, and signs, and wonders, they but ask some proof of their own puny opinions and belief; and I say unto them, these shall ye have - and should it comfort thee, thou shall be discomforted - for I say unto thee, Lay aside all thine puny opinions; seek no signs, miracles, wonders, yet ye shall seek the Light and ye shall find, for Mine hand is swift, and sure is the way, for I AM THE WAY.

I bid thee, COME follow ye Me, and I shall lead thee, and ye shall fall not!

Yet I say, thou shall not have another Master, for no man serves two masters - he either accepts Me or rejects Me.

For I am not to be second unto the dragon. I say unto them which make of Me an idol: Turn from thine idolatry, and be ye about thine preparation for the Greater part. Ye bring not thine idolatry unto Me, for I shall have none of it! NONE I say!

Ye shall surrender thineself unto me as a clean and living sacrifice; as an empty vessel which I can use; and then I shall touch thee, and I shall bless thee as thou hast not been blest.

Yea, I shall bless thee as Mine Father hast blest Me for He hast sent me with full power and knowledge and authority, that I might perform the Rite which is of Him.

I say unto thee: Make no mockery of this Rite, for thou knowest not the meaning thereof until thou hast received of Me and by Me, with the authority which HE, Mine Father, hast invested within Me, His Son - Sent of Him.

For this am I sent this day that he which so prepares himself might receive Me and of Me - by Divine Rite.

I AM HE

Sananda

THEY LOOK FOR VERIFICATION

Say unto them: The Great and Mighty Council hast been prepared for this day when the signs of the time indicates unto thee that which hast been foretold long ago. And it is present; it is the hour which wast designated within the foretelling; and man hast not read these signs, for he hast at best guessed at their meaning. And he hast plundered the sacred writ that he might form new opinions - yet he gives unto Me no credit for being within thine midst; that I am the One Sent; that I am He which wast to return.

I say they look forward to a day long in the future, while the day brings with it the fulfilling of Mine Words - the fulfilling of the prophesies. And yet they look within their ancient writ for verification; they accept not Mine sayings "this day"; they are wont to ask of Me.

They ask that I prove Mineself, without even so much as acceptance of The Word. They ask that they be shown Mine wounds! Mine poor foolish ones; Know ye that Mine wounds are yet not healed, for thou hast kept them open by thine unbelief, thine waywardness, thine thotlessness of Me, and Mine sacrifice for thee. I say: I have made the supreme sacrifice for thine sake; that ye might come to know even as I know. I say it is Mine joy when one Son is risen, when one is liberated; when one is freed from his illusion,

So be it that I am come that the illusion might pass and ye know the Truth; that ye know thine Source, thine Divinity. So be it that I bring with Me a great and mighty Force, and they are as ONE; they are of One mind, one thot.

So be it they have no other will than to serve The Father which hast sent me.

Let this be the time of great joy, for I declare unto thee, The way is prepared before thee, and the place is prepared as I have promised thee. And now, unto them which respond unto Me, I say: I am come that ye might go where I go, and ye shall be glad, for none which follow Me shall be found wanting, for I am sufficient unto thee.

Why seek ye strange gods? Why sit in the seats of the anti-christs? Why be ye luke-warm? I would have thee cold or hot! for I could then touch thee. But, O ye luke-warm Christians; I have said I shall spew thee out as the froth from the mouth of the dog; for I say the dog shall not be part of Mine flock, for the dog shall have his place - and therein is another story.

Be ye as one which can comprehend Mine sayings; be ye not a worshiper of the "Letter", for I come that we might speak unto thee as one unto the other - and the letter killeth which the Spirit makes new and resuscitates the dying.

Art thou not amongst the dying? Does thou not look unto the letter? I speak unto thee of Spirit; let the Spirit hear that which Spirit sayeth, and I shall touch thee and thine eyes shall be made to see, and thine ears made to hear.

So let it be - for I am He which speaketh unto thee which have ears.

Sananda

HIS COVENANT SHALL BE FULFILLED

Say unto them this day, that it is now come when "Mine Covenant" shall be fulfilled, and they shall be as ones prepared - for this is the end time, and it is given unto Me to be He which is Sent that the Covenant be fulfilled.

Now let it be established that this is the time for which thou hast waited; it is this day, that these things shall come to pass.

It is this day when these prophesies shall be fulfilled.

It is this day, when I shall go forth the victor over the Earth, and I shall trod underfoot everything which shall oppose Me, for I shall go forth in the manner which I have stated.

I shall go forth as One prepared to put down the oppressor - the opposer, the one which opposes the Light which I AM.

For I shall come bringing with Me Great Power, Light, and Authority, for Mine Father hast given unto Me Power and. Authority over the Earth. And now it is come when I shall proclaim, Mine Authority, for long hast he reigned which hast betrayed himself.

Now I come declaring Mine Sonship, Mine Authority, and I shall wrest from him the authority which he hast had for the many centuries wherein he hast reigned as "Prince of the World".

I say he hast reigned as "Prince of the WORLD", and now he shall be taken captive. For this I say unto thee: "Come, forsake the way of the world"; turn from him willingly and fearlessly. I see thee

75

fearful of Me; fearful to come forth and declare thineself; to give up thy legirons which hast bound thee.

Know ye not that it is by these that he holds thee fast? For hast he not promised thee a life of ease? Hast he not shown unto thee that he hast not done that which he hast led thee to believe in the days of his reign?

Hast he not delivered thee up onto the dragon which lies in wait to devour thee?

Hast he not given unto thee gall for water? Hast he not tempted thee with a life of ease and plenty?

I say unto thee, these are but his baits; he baits well his trap; he spins a delightful web and invites thee in; then thou does find thineself entrapt, knowing not how to extricate thineself.

Now I say unto thee, I ask of thee naught save obedience unto the Law; I promise unto thee not a life of ease upon the Earth; I promise thee Eternal Life - a Life of Eternal JOY!

Be ye as one free to choose this day which way ye shall go.

I come bringing with Me a Great Host which stands ready to assist thee in thine extrication from the web.

So choose ye wisely, for this is the day of salvation.

It is said: No more shall I lower Mine Light for thine sake, for when the hour strikes, I shall go as I come; as a "thief in the night I shall steal away," and no man shall see Me, for there shall be none left to see Me - for therein is another story.

So be it. I AM The Lord thy God.

Sananda

THE WORD SPEAKETH

Say unto them that all their wisdom is as foolishness of babes compared unto the wisdom of The Mighty Council.

I say unto thee: I am The Lord thy God and I am not to be found wanting.

I am the Head of The Council of which I speak, and I speak with authority. I speak knowing whereof I speak, for Mine Father hast sent Me forth as the Manifestation of The WORD - and it is for this that I say unto thee, "There is Power in The Word."

Let it be established this day that there are none which hast the Power invested within Me, for I have been sent of Mine Father that ye be lifted up - that ye might have Light - so be it and Selah.

I say it is given unto Me to be The Word made manifest. So be it. I am come into the world of flesh as THE ONE SENT - and it is for the most part not known by man what is meant by "The One Sent".

I say unto thee: They which seek the Light shall come to know, for it is said, The Light shall not be hidden from them.

It is given unto ME to see them seeking of men, and men know not wherein they are bound, for it is said they know not by which they are bound, and they ask not of Me. And for this have I said, "Seek Me out and I shall reveal Mineself unto thee." For this have I asked of thee "Come", and unto them which come, I shall prepare a table before them, and they shall eat and hunger no more.

So be it I am the provender, and I want not; therefore, I say unto thee, Come and I shall give unto thee of Mine Store, for I have Store thou knowest not of.

I say, thou hast not beheld Mine Store, for I have prepared a place wherein ye might find all thine needs supplied. Yet is it not said: Ye shall need not, want not; that all thine longing shall be no more? So let it be, and it shall be unto thee as I have said: As thou hast prepared thineself, so shall we receive - so be it the law. I am come that the Law be fulfilled.

This day I say unto thee: Let thine longing be no more; let thine sorrow be no more.

Come rejoice with Me; forsake thy way and give unto Me thine heart, thine hand, thine time, thine all, and I shall make of thee a servant.

And is it not said, "I shall exalt Mine servants over the Kings of Earth, for they shall be a Glory unto Mine Father which hast sent Me?" And these shall be as part of The Mighty Host.

I say unto all, "COME"; and unto them which so will, for therein is thine Victory.

I say Hail! Hail unto the Victor!

Sananda

THE TREASURE HOUSE

Say unto them: The Word is Holy - Holy in its Essence - for It emanates from God the Father and none shall render it inviolate. I say, it shall ever be The WORD and no man shall render it inviolate. I am now come that The Word be made known - for long hast man wondered about "THE WORD".

And at no time is it given unto man to fully comprehend It, for it originates with God - The Word was God - was with God; He spoke and THE WORD WAS.

And that wast the beginning. And who can comprehend "The Beginning", for God The Father Is The Beginning, for all things begin with Him. And like unto the beginning - He is the end, for all things which doth end, end in Him.

Prepare thineself then to return unto Him, for He is thine beginning.

Hast it not been said, He is the source of thine being?

Now ye shall become of age, and ye shall receive thine inheritance in full, and ye shall return unto the place of thine abode.

While it is said that it shall be thine own victory, I say, ye come of thine own free will - none fetch thee save thine own self will it.

Be ye of a mind to accept Me, for I AM HE; I am the One Sent that ye be brot out of bondage. So be it that I shall be unto thee thine porter; I shall say unto thee, "Pass ye in," when thou hast so prepared thineself.

Now let it be understood that none take me unawares; none pass Me unnoticed, for I am the Door Keeper. I AM THE DOOR. Let this be understood: That I AM THE LORD THY GOD, and none other is invested with the Power which is Mine. And anyone which-so-ever which attempts to enter

While thou hast said many things concerning thine opinions and preconceived ideas, I have heard no word of pity for thine own darkness or downfall. I say unto thee: O man, Thou art in a pitiful plight, for without Me thou wouldst, indeed, perish. Now I ask thee: Why rebel against Me, for am I not thine Benefactor?

Have I not given Mine all? Have I not given unto thee of Mineself that ye might go to where I go; that ye be as one made whole; made free?

I ask of thee: Why ask of man thine freedom, when they, too, are bound in body, flesh, in bondage, darkness?

I say they lead thee downward, for they have no power save it is given unto them of Me - for Mine Father hast invested within Me the Power to free thee, and it is so.

So let it suffice thee, for I AM The Lord thy God, Sent of The Father, which is The Cause of thine being.

Amen and Amen

Sananda

THE BOOK OF LIFE IS OPEN UNTO THEE

Say unto them: Mine hand is firm and Mine arm is strong, and the time is come when I shall wield the Sword which I bring.

I say: The Sword of Justice shall cut away the web of illusion; the web which holds Mine people bound. Yet, they which are bound know not by which they are bound, for the dreamer knows not that he is dreaming.

Therefore I say unto him which is bound, Awaken ye! Awaken ye all that sleepeth, for this is the day of awakening - and ye shall then know that thou hast slept the deep sleep of illusion; for think ye that ye knoweth that which goes on about thee?

Thou hast not been aware of prophesy being fulfilled this day. The time is now when these things are being done - and thou sleepeth on!

O man, thou fool! In thine illusion and conceit thou hast called thineself powerful and wise; thou hast consulted thine great and powerful men and their puny opinion, their records and the libraries of many nations - yea, even unto the archaeologists and their findings - that ye might have a glimpse of thine own nature or beginning; while I say unto thee: The Book of Life is open unto thee.

I say Come and ye stand still - denying Me the courtesy; the part of society unto which thou doest belong, would not be so rude unto one of their own kind. For I have given unto thee an invitation to come into Mine place of abode and partake of Mine Board, and I have said, "I shall open up Mine treasure chest, that ye might share

with Me Mine Inheritance which Mine Father hast willed unto Me."
Yet ye deny Me - while thou dost dine from the table prepared for
thee by the dragon.

I say unto thee: Thou art asleep; thou art as one drunken on wine
which is contaminated - contaminated I say - for he, the dragon, hast
put his filthy finger into it! He hast put his filthy finger into the wine
and contaminated it, I SAY!

Yet thou sip - and then sip some more - thinking but to sample
it, while thou dost but drink of the contamination. O foolish mortal:
Knowest thou the contamination is accumulative, and thou hast
rendered thine own self immune unto Mine Voice?

Thou knowest not Mine Voice from his - that of the dragon - for
he says, "Come"; he says, "Depart from me never"; for he is of a
mind to keep thee drunken; he is not of a mind to sober thee.

He hast given unto many a portion designed to hold them bound
- while I offer unto thee thine freedom. Yet thou hast refused to
accept Me!

Is that the way of the sober man?

I ask thee, "Is that the reasoning of a sober man?"

Thou hast feared for thineself, thine household, thine reputation,
O child of bondage! I ask of thee: What hast thou to lose? "What
hast thou to lose?" Answer ME: "WHAT HAST THOU TO LOSE?"

Naught I say! For thou hast nothing! For nothing is thine except
the one perfect gift given unto thee of The Father which has given

unto thee Being. He asks naught save that which He hast given. It is said, "A man might give his life to find it" - it is true. To give of The Father thine own will, is to find it; thine own salvation, thine own inheritance, thine own Godhood.

So be it the price HE exacts from thee. So be it the price all must pay; yet what hast thou lost? What profit a man if he gains the world and loses his soul? I ask thee, "What hast he profited by his rebellion?"

Be ye as one which can hear that which I have said. Ponder ye long upon these Mine Words - and be ye blest.

For this have I spoken this day.

Sananda

THE SPARK OF THE FIRST MAGNITUDE

Say unto them: There is within them the eternal Spark - that which is the Essence of Being, that which is the First Magnitude. And were it not for that Spark of the First Magnitude, there would not be an eternal existence, for that is the eternal part which is indestructible and without end.

Thou hast no concept of anything without end, for thou art as ones bound in darkness; bound in matter. As thou hast not as yet comprehended matter, how then canst thou lay claim unto that which is not matter?

How then canst thou fathom the endless, when thou hast not comprehended that which hast an end?

When thou hast fathomed the endless, then thou hast become the One - the One which is without end or beginning - for He alone knows the endless.

I say unto thee, "Be ye as ones prepared," for many great and wondrous things shall be revealed unto thee. And I say unto thee, put not thine hands before thine face, for it shall be shown unto them which look and listen. Therefore, I say unto thee, fear not to look; fear not to see and to listen, for it behooves thee to be alert unto that which goes on about thee.

I, too, say: I have brot thee hence, and I have placed thee in a position in which I might reach into thine wounds and heal them. I say unto thee, wherein is the thorn; wherein is the spikes that I know not, that I cannot reach?

I say unto thee: Come unto me as a little child and ask of Me, and I shall touch thee and ye shall be given that which ye have need of.

Let it suffice that I know thy needs; thine every need; So be it. I am The Lord thy God.

Such is Mine Word unto thee - and I speak unto them which have declared themself to be Mine servants.

So be it I have accepted them for their willingness to serve Me and their fellow man. So be it I say unto them: Be ye watchful and let thine hand be swift to do Mine bidding; and let thine heart bear no malice; let thine ears be quick to hear Mine Word; let thine eye behold the Glory of The Lord thy God which I AM. Praise ye the Name of Him which hast sent Me.

By His Love and Mercy I AM COME.

Sananda

ASK IN HUMBLE SUBMISSION

Say unto them: There are many which stand by to assist them, and they shall accept the assistance of these Mine servants in Mine Name - for it is given unto Me to know thine needs and thine capacity. Yet it is given unto Me to be the Director of this Host, and One shall be sent in any case wherein thou art willing to receive.

Let it be understood that the one sent shall be as one prepared, for none are sent of Me which is not prepared. I am not so foolish as to deny thee that which thou hast need of, yet that which is desired is not always that which is needful.

I am aware of the need; and that I give when asked in humble submission.

I am The Lord thy God; why deny Me, for I am the Way, the Truth and the Life.

So be ye as one submissive unto Me, and I shall show thee greater things then thou hast asked of Me, for I have within Mine hand the power to roll back the mişt which hast blinded thine mortal eyes.

I now bid thee <u>Come</u> and stand with Me; waver not for Mine firm foundation shall hold thee up. Fear not; 1 extend unto thee Mine hand; accept it and I shall lead thee, and ye shall not fall.

Hear ye Me, for I call unto thee in the manner I have chosen. I have appealed unto thee in many ways, and now I say unto thee:

Come and harken unto Mine Voice, and I shall place Mine hand upon thee, and ye shall know for a surety that I have touched thee.

So be it Mine hand shall be filled with compassion for thine frailty; yet it shall weigh heavy upon thee - and when thou hast learned the first lesson, I then shall give unto thee more. And I have not promised thee ease, for Mine servants ask nothing more than the privilege of serving Me, and to serve Me is to serve all mankind - yea, even to the lesser brothers.

Therefore I say: The reward of Mine servants shall be greater than the one which rules the world. So be ye as one satisfied to serve Me in a lowly capacity, knowing that I forget not them which serve Me. Wait upon Me, The Lord thy God, and I shall be unto thee servant, and ye shall receive double, prest down and running over, for I limit not Mine servants.

I give unto them as they are prepared to receive; according unto their capacity - and I say unto thee, I am the One which knows thine capacity; for I break not the law, I give accordingly. Yet, too, I say, As ye give so shall ye receive, for when thou hast learned to give, thou hast learned to receive - so be it the law.

I AM HE which is Sent of Mine Father that ye might increase thine capacity to receive.

Sananda

THIS IS THE WAY OF THE INITIATE

Say unto them: This is the way of the Initiate. And the Candidate first obeys the law as set forth then he finds himself as one acceptable unto the Brotherhood. And it is given unto this Brotherhood to be composed of many members which have gone the self-same way.

I say unto thee: These initiates have won their victory thru and by the same law which I have revealed unto thee. And there is none other asked of thee · no other requirements.

Let thine works be sufficient. Yet thine works without the sacrifice is as dead; is liken unto a dead carcass, and it is filled with worms, and which eateth away the carcass.

I say: Behold the dead carcass and see the filth. Works! yea, works there be - without the sacrifice. Yet I say unto thee, they scarcely are acceptable unto man; and think ye to offer unto Me thine works without the sacrifice of thine will?

O foolish man! I ask not thine plunder, thine puny possessions - I need not; I want not!

I ask of thee that which I can use - that which I can use for thine own salvation. I have said: As thou givest so shall ye receive. I ask of thee: Give unto Me thine free will that I might give it back unto thee - and then ye shall receive it with interest - compound interest!

Yea, it shall be increased many fold, for it shall bring unto thee such peace as thou hast not known.

Yea, Mine Peace I shall give unto thee. Be ye as one prepared to receive Mine Peace by giving unto Me thine <u>little</u> will, and I shall say unto thee: As thou hast been obedient in this matter, I shall give unto thee in great measure - so shall it be the day of thine surrender.

So be it I have asked of thee naught which thou canst not do; I have asked of thee little in comparison for that which ye shall receive of Me.

While it is said: Ye shall find joy in giving; it is so, for ye shall give unto Me of thine own free will. None shall force upon thee thine part which is kept for thee, for long hast it been kept. I ask of thee: Why wait longer for thine inheritance?

While it shall be kept intact, I ask of thee: Claim it in Mine Name, and for thine own sake it shall be given unto thee - as The Father hast Willed.

So let it Be.

Sananda

THE LORD ASKETH

Say unto them: While it is given unto them to walk in darkness, they are as ones bound in darkness. While it is given unto Me to know the freedom which is Mine - which is theirs for the acceptance, I say: Turn from the darkness - seek ye the Light.

Now for thine own sake I ask of thee: Accept that which is thine by Divine right, and no man shall hold thee bound.

Wherein is it said, "All that I am thou shall become." It is so; yet it is offered unto thee this day as a gift of the Father which hast given unto thee Being. Why art thou so slothful? "Why art thou so slothful?" I ask of thee!

I say: Thou art in no wise the great and wise one which thou thinkest thineself, O man, for hast thou not surrendered up thine will unto the dragon?

Hast he not betrayed thee?

Hast he given unto thee freedom?

Hast he given unto thee that which hast brot thee Peace?

I tell thee, thou hast nothing to lose by the accepting of Mine Word, Mine promise - for I betray not Mineself. How is it thou thinkest I should betray thee?

Now let us speak of the way of man - he which is fearful of Mine Way. He says unto Me, "Prove thineself. Show me thine wounds and give unto me signs and wonders that I might know thee."

While they serve the dragon, questioning him not. He gives unto them proof abundantly - yea, he gives unto them much proof that he is the deceiver, the betrayer, the tempter, and they follow him down - down - down unto their destruction.

I hear their cries even in the pit. I hear them cry for help. They cry without voice; they cry without tears, for they have seen the folly of their way; they have followed the betrayer into his own place, for he is the father of lies, and the mother of whores. He hast entrapt them, for they served him willingly. They danced the dance of the idiot's delight, while he played his five-stringed lute. I say, while he played the five-stringed lute, they danced to his tune.

I give unto them the gift which is far greater than he hast to offer, for Mine Gift is Eternal Freedom from bondage and their Eternal Sonship.

Lo, they shall cry long and loud, and they shall weary of their plight, for it is written: "They shall atone for all the misused energy; they shall seek the Light," then they shall be heard, found, and delivered out of their own free will - of their own preparation. And they shall be as ones prepared - for each unto his own preparation - each in his own environment.

While 1 say: Come - I am prepared to give unto thee assistance, and Mine assistance is given unto all which answers Me and comes of his own will. I tire not of giving Mine assistance unto them which seek to walk with Me, for I am about Mine Father's business.

Sananda

I KNOW THINE CAPACITY FOR KNOWLEDGE

Say unto them: Mine Word passeth not away - while it is given unto Me to speak that which is given unto Me to say of Mine Father which hast sent Me.

I speak and it is done; I speak and it is made manifest that which I send forth - that which I decree - for I and Mine Father is One - I and Mine Father are One. And therein is the Mystery which hast beset the men of Earth, for they know not that which hast not been revealed unto them.

While I have said Great things shall be revealed unto thee this day, this is one of the Mysteries. And after the revelation, it shall no longer be a mystery, for then ye shall bear witness of the mystery, and then ye shall know as I know.

I say unto thee, I bear witness of Mine Father which hast sent Me - now ye shall bear witness of Me, and I shall reveal unto thee the secret of thine Being.

Yet, for this thou shall prepare thineself; for it is given unto Me to know thine capacity for knowledge, and I give unto thee only as thou art prepared to receive - only as thou canst bear it.

When it is said that there is no mystery other than thine unknowing - it is so. Yet it is thine inheritance to know, for thou shall come into the fullness of thine inheritance - then ye shall be the Son returned unto thine rightful estate; then ye shall be upon the right hand of The Father, and He shall give unto thee as He hast given unto Me - Mine inheritance in full. So be it and Selah.

I say unto thee, Come and be ye as a Son returned. Share with Me the joy of thine return; stand with Me before the Throne of God and before the Twenty-four Elders, and receive of The Father thine Royal Raiment; and hear the Sons of God sing out the mighty anthem: Hail! Hail! A Son is risen! A Son is born, Rejoice! Rejoice, o ye Sons of God! Rejoice for The Son Returned. Thine ears hast not heard such glorious music, such glorious shouts of praise - and thine heart should burst for joy. Could ye this day but hear such shouts which permeate the heavens: A Son is returned! A Son hast returned victoriously! Praise The Father Solen Aum Solen!

Hail unto the Victor! Amen and Amen.

Sananda

HAIL! A SON IS BORN

Say unto them: Such is the Kingdom of Heaven! These Mine servants shall be the ones which make up the Kingdom of Heaven, for they shall be as the Sons of God which have won their Victory.

I say unto them: The ones which have won their victory is as the ones which have not yet won it, and they, too, came the same way in which I bid thee enter.

For this have I said: Come and partake of Mine joy, for do I not know the joy of victory?

It is the greatest joy when one attains his, for therein is the sacrifice; therein is the joy of seeing thine brother attain; and I say unto thee, there is no joy equal unto it. It is the greater joy when thine brother attains, for this has he finished the long journey which thou hast finished before him.

And thou hast not known the end of thine until thou hast, at last, won the last mile. Too, I say, After the last step is taken, thou but turn quickly and give unto thine brother a hand that he too might ascend the great step.

The Step is steep and strait and narrow, and it is said: Let not thine foot slip, for it is the greater fall from the height; weary not and be ye afore-warned.

I say unto the candidate: Be ye afore-warned - yet there are many which reach out a hand that ye might be assisted. Yet I say, Ye shall put forth all thine strength - all thine power and attention unto the ascent, and it shall be accomplished.

The Host stands by that nothing deter thee; to safeguard the way; to strengthen thee in thine weak parts, and to show thee wherein thou art weak. So be it that there are many which follow after thee; and after thou hast made the ascent, then ye shall be as one qualified to say unto them which follow thee: Hail! Hail unto the Victor! for thou shall know the joy of the great tidings, Hail! Hail! A Son is born!

So be it that this day the glad shouts shall go out thruout the Cosmos, and it shall be heard thruout the lands of the Earth: Hail! Hail! A Son is born!

For it is now come when many Sons shall be risen, and there shall be such joy in heaven that the echo shall be heard within the realms of the Earth, and it shall awaken man from their lethargy; and even the dead shall turn and see the onrush of the great and mighty Waters.

I say: There shall be a great and Mighty onrush of Waters, for the water of Life shall be poured out on all spirit, and it shall begin a new life. New Life shall come forth and the dead shall come to life, and they shall know there is no death - for I have spoken this day that it might be established upon the Earth as it is in Heaven. So let it be, for I AM The Lord thy God, Sent in Mine Father's Name that His will be done. So shall it be, for He hast decreed it so.

Sananda

THE SURE FOUNDATION

Say unto them: This is the time long prophesied, long foretold, when the Sons of God shall walk the Earth as ones of flesh and bone - as man.

Yet they shall not be bound by flesh, for they shall be free-born; they shall go and come at will, and they shall have free concourse into the place wherein I am. For they shall be as ones which have been unbound; no longer shall they be bound - yet they shall have the appearance of other men.

While having the appearance of other men, they shall do that which other men cannot do - and know not of - for their work shall be of the Light - they shall use the LIGHT.

They shall be as ones prepared to give unto the world a new science, a new form of Light, a new form of medicine, a new form of heat and of travel, a new form of learning which shall cause thine present methods to appear as fool's play. So be it I know, for I am of The Light, and I am come that man be lifted up - that he be brot out of his darkness.

I say: They shall resist not progress, for progress is the first order of things. Progress in the time which is now come, shall supercede anything man hast ever known.

And it is said: Man hast fallen from his high estate; for once he had a great part, and he held high the banner of Truth - and then he betrayed his trust and fell into decay.

Once again he shall fall, but from the ash he shall build again - and greater - for now it is come when he shall accept the building blocks so long rejected for the temple.

I say: Now the Temple shall be builded upon The Rock, and it shall not fall. So be it. I AM THE ROCK Which shall endure.

Sananda

PROGRESS SHALL BE THE KEY NOTE THIS DAY

Say unto them: They shall move! They shall not stand still for progress shall be the key-note this day. And without progress there is no victory, and without movement there is no progress.

Let it be understood that movement is progress, for there shall be a direction of movement this day which shall lead to progress.

Yet thou art part of the movement and seeth not the progress, neither hast thou glimpsed the victory.

While thou hast perceived the movement, thou hast not perceived the progress; thou but seeth little movement.

Hast thou not seen the movement? Hast thou not felt the progress? Yet it is slow according unto thine thinking. But think ye time is measured by three-score and ten years - even ten times ten?

I say unto thee: WE of the Great and Mighty Council see the civilizations raise and fall, and it is as the twinkling of an eye.

For it is but a moment of the Great and ALL time, for time is not measured in seasons, moons, or light-years by this Council. I say, We see that which is the fullness of The Plan; We see it as perfect.

Yet man but acts now - and of his own will - which none can calculate; not even man himself knoweth his next move - what he shall do tomorrow.

I say: It is by the acceptance of The Father's Will that he gives his sacrifice, that We of the Council hear, that his movements can be calculated; for the WILL of The Father is known unto US.

So be it man is free to choose his way at any time; then he is given a part in the Great Plan - after he hast been found trust-worthy and acceptable unto the Council, thru which The Father works.

Now I say: The Works I do ye shall do and even greater, for thou shall walk in Mine footsteps, and ye shall be as acceptable unto the Great and Mighty Council. So be it I have spoken again and I am not finished, for it is said, I am but begun. Let this be recorded for them that they might know that which I have said unto thee.

While I have said unto them: Come, and bring unto Me thine sacrifice; I, too, say, that they which prepare themself for to receive Me and of Me shall be acceptable - there shall be no discrimination, no partiality, for I say I have given unto thee the law. Thou hast obeyed. They which accept Mine Word and obey the law - make themself acceptable - shall be accepted, and they shall be given even as I have given unto thee.

I say I am no respecter of persons yet I know Mine own, for they are wont to serve one Master - one calling. They ask not of men; they ask of Me, and they are not turned away.

Seek ye the Light and ye shall find IT.

For this have I spoken

Sananda

SURELY & SWIFTLY THE HAND OF GOD MOVES

Say unto them: Behold the hand of God! Behold IT! See it move, for surely and swiftly doth it move!

I say unto thee; Surely and swiftly it moveth!

Now ye shall know the Justice of its movement, for it shall cut away all the web, the web of illusion and injustice.

I say unto thee: The novice shall be exalted over and above their masters of the "black arts", for I say unto thee, their magic spell shall be of no account unto the ones which will to follow after Me. And to them I say, Be ye of a mind to follow where I lead thee, and I shall not sacrifice thee, for I am come that ye be delivered out.

Hear ye Me and give unto Me credit for knowing the conditions within the world of men - for could thou but see the darkness and the web which hast been spun for the unsuspecting ones - the ones unaware! I tell thee, thou art blind unto that which goes on about thee; and somewhere, sometime, ye shall learn well thine lesson, and ye shall be as one prepared to see. And the veil shall be removed, and ye shall wonder at thine lethargy, for ye shall cry out for help when thou hast seen the pity of thine plight. Oh, be ye as the one which can hear and which can see! It is given unto thee to be as the blind leading the blind, for thou seest not thy plight.

I say: It is the pity of thine plight that brings near the time of great distress; and stress there shall be.

I say it is so, and they shall cry out for surcease from their grief - their pain and suffering.

Yet I say, I am sufficient unto the day. And I have said, Turn from the way of the world; seek ye the Light, and it shall not be hidden from thee.

Hear ye Me and be ye glad.

So be it I AM Sananda

WATER OF LIFE FROM THE FOUNTAINHEAD

Say unto them: This hour they shall be given that which they have fortuned unto themself, for the time is now come when they shall be given as they have sown. That which they have sown, they shall this hour reap.

And no man shall deny them their harvest, for it is theirs to claim and to reap.

They shall not deny their own sowing, for as unto the sowing, so unto the reaping. It is the law.

While it is said: Be ye alert and prepare thineself for the Greater part, it is said that ye shall turn unto Me, and I shall direct thee. It is said that I shall give unto thee the Water of Life from the Fountain Head, and it shall wash away all the dross, all the stain, and refresh and renew thine soul.

For it is now come when ye shall stand shorn of all thine laurels - all thine earthly glories. All thine success in the realm of men shall avail thee naught, for ye shall be weighed in the balance - and what shall I find? Shall I find thee wanting? Shall I find thee lacking? I say unto thee: Ye shall be found wanting!

For thou hast sown unto the wind; thou hast given unto Me no place; thou hast turned me out, while thou hast had thine temples defiled by the dragon which hast fed thee from his bitter cup.

Thou hast drunken deeply of his cup without question!

Yet thou, O mortal, asketh proof of Me!

Look ye well unto thine lot; look ye well unto thine harvest - what findest thou? What hast thou done with the energy which hast been so generously lavished upon thee in the days of thine youth?

What hast thou done with the gifts of Our Father which hast given unto us Being?

What hast thou offered up unto Him in return?

Hast thou made unto Him a sacrifice acceptable unto Him?

Know ye not that He asks of thee the only thing which is thine to give? I ask of thee, hast thou given unto Him all praise and the Glory?

O mortal man, Think ye to escape the Law? I say it is just! And for thine own sake, I stand before thee with hands tied behind Mine back - helpless to bring thee out of thine bondage, without thine own will.

Thine surrender unto Me is the Sword which cuts away Mine arm band which binds Mine hand - for I dare not enter into thine house uninvited. I trespass not; neither do I enter into the den of the dragon.

It is said: "Empty out the vessel that I might fill it," and then I shall enter in, and I shall abide with thee. And ye shall not want, neither shall ye find that thou hast been betrayed, for I am the Porter at the Gate; I keep watch over Mine own.

I say unto thee: Give unto me as I have given unto Mine Father, and ye shall receive of Me as I have received of Him.

For this am I Sent of Him

Sananda

SELF EXAMINATION

Say unto them: By Mine hand they shall be led out of bondage. By Mine own hand shall they be brot out, for I am The Lord thy God Sent of Mine Father, and no man shall stay Mine hand, for Mine arm is strong - and firm Mine hand. And it shall weigh heavy upon Mine servants, for they shall suffer persecution for Mine sake. Yet I say, great shall be their reward, for not one of Mine servants shall be forgotten or neglected.

I am not of a mind to forget Mine servants - for are they not Mine hand, Mine foot, made manifest upon the Earth? And have I not given unto them of Mineself that they be sustained - that they be blest?

I say: Blest are they that suffer persecution for Mine sake, for I am He which is come to claim Mine own - and no man shall take from Me that which is Mine.

I have said: Seek ye Me; Seek Me out, and I shall lead thee out of bondage. Yet do I not know wherein thou art bound? Do I not see thee as one bowed down with thine burdens, with thine sorrow, pain, and pity?

I, too, say: The pity of thine plight is thine lethargy, thine unknowing, thine unwillingness to follow where I lead thee. It is said, thou art a rebellious people - and it is SO!

I tell thee, Thou art a stubborn, ignorant people; thou hast set thineself up and boasted of thine power, and of thine good deeds; yet I say unto thee, Thine good deeds are overshadowed by thine bigotry, thine idolatry, thine hypocrisy, and not one shall deceive Me - for I see thee as thou art - filled with deceit and a conspiracy - and it is given unto Me to know thine motives.

O man, thou mayest deceive thineself; yet I say unto thee, "Thou deceivest Me not!" For I know that which prompts every action; I know thine motives and that which prompts each and every word, every deed!

O man, I say unto thee: Search well thine heart; search well thine closet; search well thine garments - let no blood be found on thine own garments. Wash not thine hands and bring unto Me the bowl to prove thineself. For I say unto thee: I look not unto the bowl - I look at thine heart!

And what do I find there? I say unto thee: Purify thineself! Cleanse out thine own closet, cleanse thine own garments, and cleanse thine hands, and make thineself a fit and profitable servant - and I shall take note of thee.

I say: Ye enter not into Mine place of abode unprepared. Be ye up and about thine preparation, O ye laggards! I am speaking that ye be awakened; thou shall not be kept in darkness when ye seek The Light which I AM.

I AM HE which is Come that ye awaken.

So be it I AM The Lord thy God.

Sananda

THE CALL

Say unto them: The Lord thy God hast spoken, and it is given unto Him to be the Director of this New Dispensation. And it is for this dispensation that He hast opened up the way, that those which hear His Voice might come unto Him and receive of Him, even as thou hast received.

I say unto thee: The way hast not been easy - yet I promised thee not ease, for I asked thee what thine choice was, and thou chose to follow Me - for this have I chosen thee from them.

I have called thee; thou hast answered Me and been the obedient servant which I have commanded thee.

Now it is said that as thou hast prepared thineself, so shall ye receive; yet they which seek lengthy sermons or flowery speech, are liken unto the empty bowl which hast within it a leak.

They are not solid - they are shallow and fragile; they have to be handled with care!

I say unto thee: Thou art as the rock, and thou art of the mind to follow where I lead thee. And it is given unto thee to be as one within their places of defecation, yet thou art no part of it.

Thou asketh not for their approval; their favors; their opinions, for thou art of Mine house. For I have accepted thee as a trustworthy servant; I have given unto thee the key unto Mine house wherein ye might enter in and abide with Me.

I am not so foolish as to give unto them the key unto Mine abode until they have proven themself.

I say unto thee: Pass ye in and abide with Me, Mine faithful servant, for thou hast proven thineself trustworthy.

Blest art they which prove their worth.

I AM The Lord Thy God.

SACRIFICE IS REQUIRED

Say unto them: By their own efforts are they saved. Yet, works alone are not sufficient unto salvation.

I say all their good works are not sufficient unto their salvation.

Yet without good works they are lost. While the intent might be present, the work hast not been done. I say, Works is not sufficient - and their faith is not sufficient. While faith without works is dead, works without that selfless sacrifice is dead - of no account - for the sacrifice is required of thee; thy free will. O man, when wilt thou heed that which I say unto thee? Listen, o man! Listen!! For I speak unto thee of important things which thou hast not heard.

I say: All thine "Good Works" are not sufficient unto salvation. Thou hast not believed in Me, neither Mine Word sufficiently to follow after Me. I say, Ye shall follow where I lead thee, and I shall direct thee aright, and ye shall find in Me a friend trustworthy, for I shall not betray thine trust.

I say, thine trust in Me shall be justified. Have I not said, prove Me and ye shall be glad?

For thine faith in Me shall ye follow Me; yet, wherein hast thou forsaken father, mother, sister, brother, children, home, comfort, society, position and creed, dogmas; last but not least, thine own self-esteem, thine own opinions of self-love, of self- gratification?

I ask of thee: Wherein is thine willingness. Wherein is thine sacrifice?

Wherein is thine submission unto Me? Wherein is the reward? Wherein is the glory?

I say unto thee: The glory shall be short-lived; it shall be as the pit, for it shall be as black as the night before thee, and ye shall fail to find it rewarding, for it shall be as ash in thine hand. So be it I have spoken unto them which have ears to hear, for none other can hear; the ones without ears cannot hear; the ones without will cannot surrender it up. The ones without surrender cannot enter into the Holy of Holies - so be it I know of which I speak.

Let it suffice that I AM The Lord thy God.

Sananda

HAVE PAID A PRINCELY RANSOM

Say unto them: The way of The Lord is strait and narrow; the way is open unto them, and it is given unto Me to be the Wayshower. And there is but one DOOR - which I AM - which leads unto Mine father's House, from whence thou hast gone forth.

I say: I AM THE DOOR thru which thou shall enter therein; why then rebel against Me, The Lord thy God?

Why then follow after strange gods? Why then forfeit the ransom which I have paid for thine freedom?

I say, I have paid a princely ransom for thine sake; why then refuse Mine offer this day?

I say unto thee: I stand before thee as one prepared to deliver thee out of bondage, Hast thou heard that which I have said? Hast thou lifted up thine feet? Hast thou lifted thine hand? Hast thou opened thine mouth that ye might prove Me? Hast thou offered up unto Me thineself, thine heart, thine will? Hast thou made any sacrifice whatsoever, in Mine Name?

Hast thou given unto Me credit for being that which am? Hast thou given unto Me credit for knowing thine weakness, thine needs, and knowing wherein thine strength lies? Hast thou been true unto thineself? Hast thou answered Mine call? Hast thou been as one humble of heart? Such I would ask of thee; such I would have thee ask of thine own self.

Wherein hast thou found peace? Wherein hast thou found surcease from thine labors, thine suffering? Wherein hast thou loved thine neighbor as thineself; wherein hast thou served the Lord thy God with all thine heart, all thine strength? Wherein hast thou been obedient unto the Law which I have given unto thee; wherein hast thou followed in Mine footsteps?

I say unto thee: These are the things I would have thee ask of thineself; and examine well thine hands, and see what thou hast upon them!

Let not the sins of another be found upon thine own hands. I say unto thee, thou art not responsible for the "sins" of another!

Look well unto thine own short-comings, and be ye as one blameless before Me, and I shall give unto thee that which I have for thee.

Yet ye shall cleanse out the old wine, and I shall put therein new which shall invigorate and refresh thee. So be it I hold within Mine hand the Cup which I shall proffer unto thee, when thou hast prepared thineself.

So be it I AM HE which is Sent of Mine Father; as thou hast accepted Me, so hast thou accepted HIM, for Mine Father and I are ONE.

So shall it ever Be - worlds without end.

Amen and Selah.

Sananda

NO PROTECTION IN ARMAMENT

Say unto them: While it is not the part of all men to go into battle, it is given unto others, and for this is it said, As thou art prepared so shall ye receive.

Now it is given unto Me to see them bearing arms for their own protection - for their own protection? I ask?

Wherein is their protection; wherein have they fortuned unto themself protection?

I say there is no protection in their arms - their armament. Let it be that which it will; they shall find no protection therein. It shall be as naught, for ever greater shall be their skill; their talent which shall go for naught.

I say of them which giveth unto the dragon of his energy, time, and talent, shall be as one cast down, for it is said: Be ye alert and follow him not into the pit, for surely he but leads thee downward into the pit!

I ask of thee, O man: Wherein hast it profited thee to arm thineself? O thee of little knowledge, I say unto thee: Thou knowest not the law, and thou hast not bothered thineself to learn the law -

The LAW by which ye shall be saved.

I tell thee: By the Law art thou saved. Obey ye the law and thou shall have no fear. Fear of man is thine lot - fear of the unknown. O man, wherein is thine safety?

Surely not in thine armaments; surely not in thine treaties; surely not within thine own wisdom;

Surely not within thine own strength;

Surely not within thine own household;

For is it not given unto thee to be first betrayed by thine own household? Are they not first to turn thee out when thou hast but declared thineself Mine Disciple? | say, they are first to deny thee.

Yet I say: Come ye out from amongst them and follow ye Me, and I shall give unto thee the protection of Mine garment, for I shall make a Shield of Mine Cloak for thee; I shall spread Mine Mantle about thee and I shall protect thee and remember thee all the days of thine life.

I say: Arise from thine lethargy; come ye out from amongst them which blaspheme Mine Name. Magnify the Name of The Lord thy God; glorify The Father as He hast glorified Me. I say, Come! And be ye as one responsible for thine own salvation, for no man giveth it or taketh it away. I bid thee, follow ye Me, and partake of Mine garner, and I shall give unto thee as thou hast not received.

So be it that I am prepared to go all the way with thee - even unto the end, for I am come that ye be lifted up.

Let it BE as The Father hast Willed it.

Amen.

Sananda

THIS IS THE WORD OF GOD

Say unto them: This is the way; this is the Word of God; and by the Word they shall be made whole. So be it that there is no other way - no other word by which they are made whole.

By the WORD of The Father Almighty God thou art made whole - by no other means.

So be it I am The Lord thy God, and I declare unto thee there is no other means by which thou art made whole - perfect - and by no other door do ye enter into the Holy of Holies, other than this Door which I AM.

For Mine father hast sent me that ye be brot out of bondage, and none other shall usurp the part which He hast given unto Me.

Yet by His Grace and Mercy hast He sent Me, and according unto the Word am | come. I am come according unto the Word, and that the Law be fulfilled. i come not to set aside the Law - rather that it be fulfilled this day.

Be ye as ones prepared to receive that which I bring, for I say unto thee, I bring with Me great Light and power. I bring with Me the rod, which is the rod of power, and it shall be as the authority of The Father which hast sent Me.

And at no time shall any man take from Me that rod, for 1 yield not Mine authority, Mine position, Mine post of authority. For He, The Father, hast prepared Me for this part, for I am His servant, His hand, His foot, and I am His Will made manifest, I have no other will.

I AM the manifestation of His Will. This I KNOW.

And it is said that ye, too, shall come to know even as 1 know. This shall be as He wills it - and as thou hast made the supreme sacrifice. When thou hast surrendered thine will unto Him, then I shall give unto thee that which He hast given unto Me for thee, and it shall be thine by inheritance. Yet ye shall receive it thru Me and by Mine Grace, for I have come unto thee that ye might know; that ye might prepare thineself for to receive thine inheritance. And it is by Mine Grace that ye shall be prepared; for I have prodded thee, I have given of Mineself in selfless service that ye be prepared; I have declared unto thee the Law. I have walked the Earth in flesh that I might do so; I have given unto thee miracles, signs, and wonders, yet ye clamor for more!

Think ye that I am not The Lord of Lords, the Host of Hosts? Think ye that I need prove Mineself unto thee?

I say unto thee, o man of Earth: I am not One to give unto thee the miracles thou asketh to please thine fancy; that ye might speak lightly of thine experience; or that ye might speak knowingly unto thine neighbor of thine experience. I say there is a purpose in Mine Work, in Mine manifestations. Have 1 not manifested Mineself unto Mine Priestess before a company? Wherein are they? Wherein have they become witness of Me? Wherein have they borne testimony of Mine coming? Wherein have they given unto Me credit for being He which is Sent? Wherein do I find them eating and drinking? Yea,

I find them eating of the carcass, drinking of the wine, and finding therein great merriment - and they call it joy!

So be it that they have betrayed themself, for I came bearing the Arms of Freedom - Freedom's Arms. I stood before them as one of flesh and bone; I reached out a hand unto them in great compassion - and did they accept it? I say unto thee: They knew Me not! Now they ask for miracles! I say, poor foolish mortals - they see and they know not that which they see; they ask and they receive not that which they are given. I say they are not as yet prepared to receive Me or of Me. So be it they shall prepare themself, then I shall show Mineself, and they shall come to know. I shall not tire of them. While I do weary of their foolishness - I wait.

So be it I have one which hast accepted Me, and for this do I now speak thusly; and I say I am glad that I am privileged to do so, for by this one's grace is it made possible. So be it I shall, speak until I am finished, and no man shall set his hand unto Mine mouth.

For I AM The Lord thy God.

Sananda

I AM THE SOLE HEIR OF THIS STATION

Say unto them: Mine hand shall rest heavy upon them, and they shall be as ones aware of it.

Yet I say, I come not to soothe them; I come that they be prepared. I say, they know not that which is before them, yet they have been warned many times. They have been given signs, and they have been given the law - and the milestones are clearly marked - likewise, the pitfalls!

I say the pitfalls are marked well, for I have clearly and fearlessly pointed them out unto thee. I have gone over the path which thine feet now tread, and I have measured it inch by inch, mile by mile, and I have given unto thee instructions how to walk "The Path"; where to place thine foot. I have said unto thee: Walk ye in Mine footsteps, and ye shall find solid ground. I say, Ye shall find the firm ground, and it shall be given unto thee to go where I lead thee.

Let it be said that I, The Lord thy God, hast come into flesh for the purpose of preparing the way before thee. While this is so, I gave of Mineself freely and fearlessly without stint. For Mine Love I gave of Mineself, and I have received Mine reward while asking not; asking no other reward than the privilege of serving Mine Father's Will.

For this have I received Mine Inheritance in full - for it is given unto Me to have Mine reward. And I say unto thee, Thou are no less than I, for there is no difference within us, save I am Mine Father's

Son by reason that I am the Sole Heir of this Station - this part which He hast Willed unto Me - and I shall not yield it up unto another.

Yet each hast a part; no two are alike, no two the same. Yet I say, when one asks, he shall be given as he is prepared to receive. And if he betrays himself, another shall be raised up, and he shall perform the duties of the office appointed unto him which betrayed his trust - and himself.

While it is said, Woe unto the one which betrays himself; too, it is said, "Many are called and few are chosen." And each which is chosen shall account for themself; they shall be tried and found trustworthy. I say none other are chosen, for I am not so foolish as to give of Mine store unto the foolish which know not its worth.

I say, Behold ye the Glory of The Lord thy God, for stand at the Door and knock, and blest is he which opens unto Me, for I shall enter in and abide with him.

So be it I AM HE which is Sent.

Sananda

EACH UNTO HIS OWN TONGUE

Say unto them: Be ye as a willing servant, and ye shall be given in great measure - and it is so. For I say unto thee: I forget not Mine servants, for are they not Mine hands and Mine feet made manifest upon the Earth? Do I not do a work thru them that cannot be done without them?

Now I say: It is for the ones that I shall bring forth that the Kingdom of God shall be established upon the Earth. And without their sacrifice of the will, I could not perform the works which shall be done this day. And it shall be given unto this generation to know the power of the Word and the purity of the Word for it shall proceed forth as a two-edged Sword, and it shall be as power - as the Power of God Almighty - and as nothing man hast known. For he shall be as one lifted up, as one arisen, and he shall be given the power and authority to speak the Word, and it shall be unto all men all things; for each unto his own tongue; each unto his own understanding.

While I have said I shall lift up a generation which shall bring about a mighty work, I say it shall not be as man hast thot, not as he hast fancied, not as he hast opinioned. For it shall be as no man hast envisioned, for it shall be as God The Father Wills it - and who amongst thee knows that which HE shall do?

I say unto thee: Know ye not that thou hast not dreamed of His Plan. Thou hast not dreamed what thou shall yet become. I say unto thee: Arise! Shake off thine legirons; step forth and declare thineself; prepare thineself to meet The Lord thy God, and I shall show Mineself unto thee.

121

I say, Prove thineself and I shall do likewise, for I am not fearful. I am just speaking out that ye might know that which is lawful. So be it for thy sake that I speak. Be ye wise and keep thine house in order that I might enter in, and I shall abide with thee. Hear ye Me and give unto Me credit for knowing that which I say unto thee, for I am that I AM.

And for that do I send unto thee Mine servant that ye might receive of Me. Deny not Mine servant, and then I shall accept thee and thine gift. But offer not thine gifts unto Me while thou dost deny Mine servant, for I have given unto this one the gift, and it hast been accepted in Mine Name.

So be it this one hast served Me faithfully and fearlessly; be not so foolish as to spit upon the Word which I give for thee, for knowest thou thine time is come to account for thine acts? And no man shall atone for thee.

Let it profit thee to seek.

The LIGHT which I AM.

Sananda

I AM APT IN MINE PART

Say unto them: Behold in Me The Light; behold in thineself the Light; walk ye in the Light Be ye as one which hast thine hand in Mine, and I shall direct thee in all thine ways. I am come that ye be led out of bondage, and I am sufficient unto thee - I am apt; I am apt in Mine part; I am prepared by Mine Father which hast sent Me. He hast given unto Me the authority and power to do that which He Wills Me to do, and I shall not betray Mineself, for I come that HIS WILL be done - and at no time shall I fail.

Now be ye as one which hast the will to follow Me, for I shall be unto thee all that ye have need of; I shall give unto thee as thou art prepared to receive - and therein is wisdom.

Let the hand which hast fortuned unto thee Life, be blest by thee, in thee, and glorify The Father which is the Giver of Life - and therein is thine reward. Praise ye the Name of The Father Solen Aum Solen; hear ye that which I say unto thee and ye shall be blest. Hast it not been said: Cleanse out the vessel that I might fill it?

Hast it not been said: Take upon thineself Mine yoke? And hast it not been said: Ye shall walk in the way in which ye should go?

I tell thee of a surety: I have pointed the way; I shall lead thee aright. I shall sustain thee in thine sojourn; I shall deliver thee out surely and safely, for I AM The Lord thy God.

So be it I AM HE, The One Sent.

Sananda

THE ROD OF POWER

Say unto them: Mine Word shall go forth as a mighty Rod - as Power - and it shall be as nothing known by man before, for man shall come to know the Word which shall be as the two-edged Sword. And it shall cut loose the web which hast bound man; which hast been unto him his bounds. And he shall know no bounds, for he shall be freed from his bounds - the bounds which hast bound him fast.

Let this day be the fulfillment of the Word, for it is so decreed.

My Word shall be The Father's Will, for HE hast placed within Mine hand the Rod of power which is His Will. The power shall be without limit, and it shall be given unto Me to know that which is given unto Me to do.

I shall go forth as a mighty power. I shall do that which no man hast done. I shall pick from amongst them Mine people, and I shall place them in the place which is prepared for them. And I shall prepare them for a work yet unknown unto them, for have I not said, "As they are prepared so shall they receive"? And it is the Law.

Now, within the place wherein I shall place them, they shall receive in greater measure, and they shall then be as ones prepared for a greater part. Yet no man can say what that part shall be, for that is not revealed unto any man - for it shall be unto them secret. They shall not be given that either by revelation or intuition, until they have prepared themself and proven themself. Then they shall be given the plan; then they shall make their own choice where they shall serve - and in what capacity. Then they shall know the wisdom of waiting, for no man seeth the whole plan; and to choose while in darkness is as the blind man going forth without understanding of the service unto the plan to sow his fields without the grain, for he is void of understanding - and he hast not the wisdom to choose, in his ignorance of the plan.

Yet within the place wherein he shall be put, he shall review the records, and he shall see that which he hast done, that which he can do; that which he hast prepared himself for to do, and he shall then be qualified to make a choice, and wisely. So let him this day follow Me and I shall lead him aright.

For I AM The Lord thy God.

Sananda

SWEAR NO ALLEGIANCE

Say unto them: They shall first seek the Light and they shall find; they shall find that which they seek. Yet they shall find that when they seek of men, they shall find sorrow and disillusion; they shall not be satisfied; they shall not find joy, for man is as yet not filled with Light - they walk in darkness, and they are not, at the present, prepared to comprehend the Light which I AM.

I say unto them: Swear no allegiance unto any man; any nation; any thing. Be ye as one free to follow in Mine footsteps, and I shall ask naught of thee, save obedience unto the Law.

Let it profit thee to hear that which I have said unto thee, for I am come that ye might be blest.

So be it I AM The Lord thy God.

Sananda

CHANGE NOT THE WORD

Say unto them: Say it as it is said unto thee, for there is not one that shall change it or deny it, for the better. For it shall be given unto the one which changes the Word or places his own ideas and opinions upon it, to suffer the consequence.

I say unto them: I make not the Law, I abide by it. And it is Mine part to warn thee: Be ye not so foolish! For ! am The Lord thy God, and I have spoken for the good of all mankind. And it is given unto Me to know their needs, their short-comings, their want; and I am come that they might receive in greater measure. So be it I speak in simple language that they might know that which I say. Let them which are of a mind, come unto Me, and I shall touch them and they shall know.

So be it I AM The Lord thy God, Sent of Mine Father, The Source of Thine Being.

Sananda

I AM HE WHICH HAST OVERCOME FLESH

Say unto them: They shall arise as from the tomb; they shall put on new garments, and they shall be as ones made new; they shall be as ones unbound, and then they shall know Me as I know them, and no man shall be unto them a porter - for I say unto them, they shall be free to go and come at will - there shall be no barriers.

I say: This is freedom!

And wherein is the man which is free in the flesh of Earth? I say flesh binds him, for he comes under the law of Earth - and mortal flesh belongs to the Earth, for it is Earth substance - of the Earth, earthy.

I am He which hast overcome flesh; 1 no longer come under the law of flesh, for I am He which is risen, and I am come this day as The Risen Christ. I am no longer bound unto the Earth nor her limitations. I know no limitation, for I am free, and I and Mine Father are One.

Now it is come when many shall be unbound, and they shall be forever free from the law of Earth - for they shall be as ones prepared to walk the Royal Road even as l. 1 say, even as I, for this have I labored with them. Now ye shall close this account with these Mine Words unto them: Be ye as ones prepared to go where I go, for! go unto Mine Father which hast sent Me.

I AM The Lord thy God.

Sananda

THE SCRIBE

Hear ye Mine Beloved, this Mine Word which I speak unto thee, for it is for thee that I speak. Yet it shall profit them to know that which I say unto thee - for it is for thine grace and thine obedience that I give unto them.

And it is now come when the foregoing parts shall be placed together, and placed in one volume; and they shall be bound as one and given unto anyone who-so-ever wills to have them. Yet they shall not be forced upon any man - anyone who-so-ever might not care to receive them.

These parts shall not be sold or put aside, for not any one can say the result thereof. For it is given unto Me to know these words to be Mine - and wherein is there one which can make of Me a liar, or a poor Spirit within darkness?

I say, I am not in darkness, neither am I of the dead; I am The Risen Christ - I have received Mine inheritance in full. So be it I come that all men be lifted up; so let them accept Mine Word and Mine servant, then I shall give unto them in greater measure.

So be it I have fortuned unto them that which they are capable of receiving. Let their capacity be increased, and I shall give unto them in greater measure - prest down and running over.

Such is Mine Word unto thee concerning these Words, here in this part. For that matter, I shall give unto thee in a greater measure as a reward for service rendered. So be it I place upon thee Mine hand, and I say unto thee: "Well done Mine faithful servant."

I AM The Lord thy God.

So be it and Amen.

Sananda

O, FATHER - BLESSED ART THOU

O, Holy Father, Father of Mine Being - Giver of Life art Thou. O Father, this day I would that they - these THINE Children KNEW Thee as I do ---

Let it BE.. For this have I revealed Mineself ---

Father - Blessed Art Thou - Holy Art Thou - and Mighty is Thine Works. PERFECT ART Thine Works ---

Keep these Thine Children - in the Way Thou would that they go. Hold them Father - I ask it for their sake ---

Thou knowest them and their every need. Yet I speak that they might bear witness of Mine Love - Which I bear for them. For their sake have I beared Mine Cross. For their sake have I lowered Mine Light - that they might see that which they are capable of comprehending ---

Give unto them greater capacity or knowledge - O Father, Let them arise with Me - and return unto their rightful estate - that which Thou hast Willed unto them ---

Thank Thee O Blessed Father - that Thou hast heard Me. I bless them with Mine Presence ---

SO LET IT BE

I AM THINE SON

Sananda

www.ingramcontent.com/pod-product-compliance
Lightning Source LLC
Chambersburg PA
CBHW070808050426
42452CB00011B/1953